SPOTLIGHT

CHATTANOOGA & KNOXVILLE

MARGARET LITTMAN

Contents

CHATTANOOGA & KNOXVILLE

CHATTANOOGA AND THE OVERHILL COUNTRY

Nicknamed the Scenic City, Chattanooga, the smallest of Tennessee's four main cities, is also regarded as its most livable. In 2011 *Outside* magazine's readers named it their "ultimate dream city." Perched on the bank of the Tennessee River, surrounded by mountains, Chattanooga was once an industrial powerhouse. After some hardscrabble years, now it is a model for urban ecofriendly redevelopment. City parks, a pedestrian bridge, free downtown (electric, zero-emission) buses, and an abundance of nearby recreation have brought people back downtown. Its arts district is anchored by a museum with one of the best collections of American art in the South. The University of Tennessee has a downtown Chattanooga campus, which lends an additional youthful energy to the city.

In addition, Chattanooga is one of the best destinations for families in Tennessee. Perhaps with the exception of the Great Smoky Mountains, no other part of Tennessee has as much to offer its pint-size visitors. The Tennessee Aquarium is its flagship attraction, but there is also a downtown IMAX theater, the Chattanooga Zoo, and railroad excursions. On Lookout Mountain, families will enjoy riding the Incline Railroad, going beneath the earth to see the hard-to-describe Ruby Falls, and exploring the fairyland-style rock gardens at Rock City. On top of this are downtown parks, the local AA baseball team, nearby Lake

© MELINDA FAWVER/123RF

HIGHLIGHTS

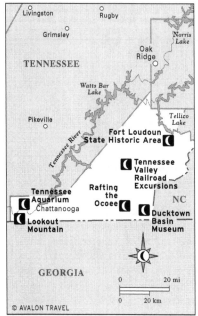

◖ **Tennessee Aquarium:** See freshwater and ocean creatures up close at one of the best aquariums in the country (page 13).

◖ **Lookout Mountain:** This narrow finger of the Cumberland Plateau offers great views as well as Rock City, Ruby Falls, and the setting of a Civil War battle (page 16).

◖ **Rafting the Ocoee:** High-velocity rapids keep even the most experienced paddlers at the edge of their rafts on a journey down the Ocoee River (page 36).

◖ **Ducktown Basin Museum:** Learn about the legacy of copper mining at this top-notch, yet down-home, museum (page 39).

◖ **Tennessee Valley Railroad Excursions:** All aboard! See old mining towns and beautiful mountain passes on a scenic railroad ride (page 44).

◖ **Fort Loudoun State Historic Area:** The complex dynamics of the Tennessee frontier come to life at this re-created 18th-century British fort (page 49).

LOOK FOR ◖ TO FIND RECOMMENDED SIGHTS, ACTIVITIES, DINING, AND LODGING.

Winnepesauka, and an amusement park, not to mention lots of hiking, paddling, and other outdoor activities.

The nearby Overhill region in southeastern Tennessee is a region of natural beauty and rich heritage. Five rivers wind down the mountains and through the valleys here, with names—Hiwassee, Ocoee, Tellico, Conasauga, and Tennessee—that trace back to the Overhill Cherokee people. The Ocoee's white-water rapids attract rafters and kayakers; the calms of the Hiwassee are a refuge for Sandhill crane and other waterfowl.

The foothill country here is dotted with towns and landmarks named in the Cherokee language, and others—like Reliance, Copperhill, and Cleveland—that are linked to lives and industries of more modern settlers. Museums in Ducktown, Etowah, and Englewood preserve the stories of Tennesseans who earned their livelihoods in the mines, on the railroads, and in the textile factories of East Tennessee.

It is the natural beauty of the region that is its greatest calling card, however. The Cherokee National Forest contains hiking trails, bike paths, lakes, and rivers. The landscape invites you to slow down and enjoy the seasons and the gentle passage of time. For more to do near Chattanooga, Monteagle and Sewanee are good places to visit.

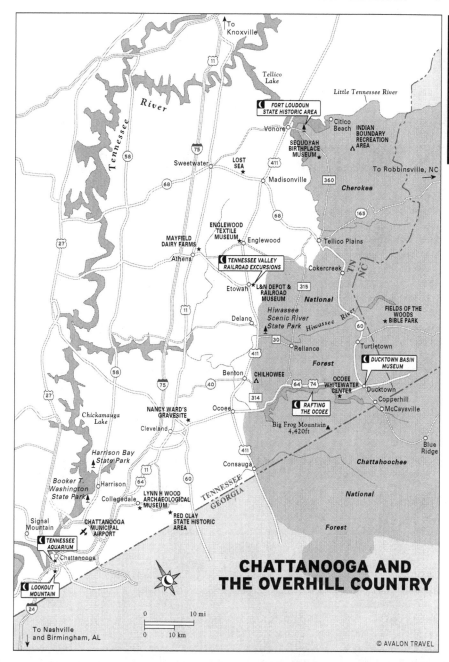

To Knoxville

Tennessee River

Tellico Lake

Little Tennessee River

FORT LOUDOUN STATE HISTORIC AREA

Citico Beach

INDIAN BOUNDARY RECREATION AREA

Vonore

SEQUOYAH BIRTHPLACE MUSEUM

Sweetwater

LOST SEA

Madisonville

To Robbinsville, NC

Cherokee

ENGLEWOOD TEXTILE MUSEUM

Englewood

Tellico Plains

MAYFIELD DAIRY FARMS

Athens

TENNESSEE VALLEY RAILROAD EXCURSIONS

Cokercreek

Etowah

L&N DEPOT & RAILROAD MUSEUM

National

FIELDS OF THE WOODS BIBLE PARK

Delano

Hiwassee Scenic River State Park

Hiwassee River

Reliance

Turtletown

DUCKTOWN BASIN MUSEUM

Benton

CHILHOWEE

Forest

OCOEE WHITEWATER CENTER

Ducktown

Ocoee

RAFTING THE OCOEE

Copperhill

McCaysville

NANCY WARD'S GRAVESITE

Big Frog Mountain 4,420ft

Chickamauga Lake

Cleveland

Chattahoochee

Blue Ridge

Harrison Bay State Park

Consauga

National

Booker T. Washington State Park

Harrison

LYNN H WOOD ARCHAEOLOGICAL MUSEUM

Collegedale

TENNESSEE
GEORGIA

Forest

Signal Mountain

CHATTANOOGA MUNICIPAL AIRPORT

RED CLAY STATE HISTORIC AREA

TENNESSEE AQUARIUM

Chattanooga

LOOKOUT MOUNTAIN

CHATTANOOGA AND THE OVERHILL COUNTRY

0   10 mi

0   10 km

To Nashville and Birmingham, AL

© AVALON TRAVEL

PLANNING YOUR TIME

This region of the state is perfect for a two-in-one vacation: Start with three days in Chattanooga and follow it with three days in the Overhill region. It's a plan that offers a nice balance of urban sophistication and outdoor exploration, and can be an ideal family vacation. If you have more time, add a day in Monteagle and Sewanee (in the Cumberland Plateau).

If you have only a long weekend and pine for the outdoors, cut your time in Chattanooga to two days and spend your third day at the Ocoee River.

Remember that many attractions in Chattanooga—such as the aquarium—may be very crowded during summer weekends.

Chattanooga

Cradled in a tight bend of the Tennessee River, Chattanooga is a city that has risen from the ashes. Chattanooga's first boom was after the Civil War, when industry and transportation flourished. Expansive warehouses and railway yards bustled with activity, and the city that grew up around them was lively and sophisticated.

Chattanooga's prosperity was not to last, however. By the 1970s and '80s, the Scenic City was dirty, dilapidated, and nearly deserted by all but the most loyal residents.

Chattanooga's turnaround is one of the great stories of the success of urban planning and downtown development. Starting with the flagship Tennessee Aquarium in the early 1990s, Chattanooga has flourished with the addition of new attractions. Planners have also emphasized quality of life for residents; Chattanooga is pedestrian friendly, easy to navigate, and boasts several lovely downtown parks.

History

Chattanooga's location in the bend of the Tennessee River made it secure, temperate, and fertile. Native Americans are believed to have settled here more than 8,000 years ago. The Cherokee called the area *Chado-na-ugsa* (rock that comes to a point), referring to nearby Lookout Mountain.

After the forced removal of the Cherokee, settlers established Ross's Landing, a trading post on the river. In 1839, the town of Chattanooga was incorporated. Eleven years later, the first rail line, the Western and Atlantic, arrived in the city.

Chattanooga was called the city where cotton meets corn. It was the gateway to the Deep South. Goods passed through Chattanooga whether by rail or river, giving rise to a massive warehouse and transportation industry. Residents here were sympathetic with the Confederate view, even before the State of Tennessee voted to secede from the Union in 1861.

Chattanooga was of great strategic importance during the Civil War. Confederates moved in to defend her in 1861, and for the first two years of the war Chattanooga was an important supply depot for the Southern states. In the fall of 1863, after the bloody battles of Chickamauga and Chattanooga, the city was in Federal hands. Once again, Chattanooga's infrastructure and strategic position proved useful to its occupiers. Sherman used Chattanooga as a staging point for his march through Georgia and South Carolina, and Union troops built warehouses, stockyards, and hospitals to support the army.

After the Civil War, northern industrialists sought to capitalize on Chattanooga's location, infrastructure, and proximity to natural resources. These industrialists were also the political leaders of the city, and they relied heavily on the political support of newly enfranchised African Americans. During this period,

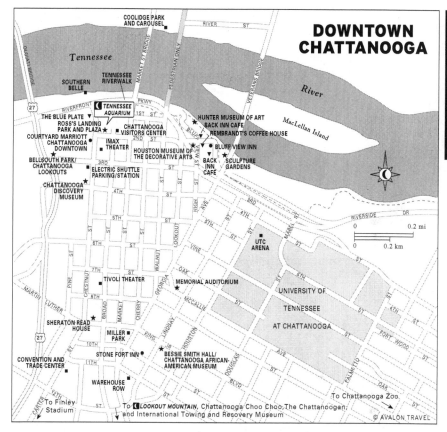

DOWNTOWN CHATTANOOGA

African Americans were elected to local office, established businesses, and pursued education.

Economic woes of the 1890s, combined with the social and political backlash against postwar policies that empowered African Americans, led to hard times for the city's blacks. Jim Crow arrived in Chattanooga and would remain until the civil rights movement of the 1950s and '60s.

Chattanooga remained a city based on industry and manufacturing. In 1899 the city secured exclusive bottling rights to Coca-Cola, and the Chattanooga Coca-Cola bottling plant grew into one of the city's largest and most successful businesses. (Coke still rules the beverage counters in town today. You might also find an RC, but likely not a Pepsi.) After the Tennessee Valley Authority built dams, increased electricity supply, and eased flooding during the 1930s and '40s, Chattanooga experienced another boom, further bolstered by World War II. The economic success was not without problems, however. By the late 1960s Chattanooga was one of the most polluted cities in America.

Over the past two decades, Chattanooga has experienced an exciting period of rebirth. In 2008 Volkswagen Group of America announced that it was putting its U.S. headquarters in the city, a move that lead to building a $1 billion green assembly plant. Spurred by the success of the Tennessee Aquarium, downtown Chattanooga is once again alive. Pedestrian walkways and good public transportation help make the city a pleasant place to be, while its lovely location on the bank of the Tennessee makes it distinctive.

Orientation

Chattanooga is defined and confined by its geography. The city sits in the bend of the Tennessee River and is hemmed in by mountains on three sides. Missionary Ridge, which runs along the fourth side, was a barrier for earlier residents, but now tunnels pass through it.

The best place to get an understanding of Chattanooga's setting is from atop Lookout Mountain, where you can see the Cumberland Plateau, the Tennessee River, and Missionary Ridge.

DOWNTOWN

Market Street and **Broad Street** are the two major north–south thoroughfares downtown. Market Street continues across the river via the Market Street Bridge; Broad Street dead-ends in front of the aquarium. Cross streets 1st–9th make navigation simple.

South and east of the aquarium district is the city's business and government center. Here you will find large office buildings; city, state, and federal offices; the University of Tennessee; the city's African American museum; and Warner Park, home of the Chattanooga Zoo.

Market Street Bridge

© MELINDA FAWVER/123RF

Farther south is the world-famous Choo Choo and Chattanooga's old commercial district, centered along **Main Street.** Explore around the Choo Choo, and you will see lots of old brick buildings that once housed warehouses, hotels, and manufacturers that needed to be near the railroad. Many of these buildings have been restored and now house new businesses; some still sit empty.

Bluff View is a smattering of elegant old homes located about three blocks east of the aquarium, along the river, with, as its name suggests, a view from the bluff over the river. The city's art museum is here, along with a collection of outstanding restaurants. You can get to Bluff View on foot either by walking about four blocks along 3rd Street from downtown, along the Riverwalk boardwalk that follows the river, or across the remarkable Holmberg pedestrian bridge, a 250-foot lighted glass bridge that connects the south end of Walnut Street to Bluff View.

Across the river from downtown is the **Northside.** Accessible by car via the Market Street Bridge or by foot along the Walnut Street pedestrian bridge, Northside is a dining, shopping, and entertainment center with a fresher, more youthful feel than downtown. Coolidge Park along the waterfront is another attraction on this side of the river.

LOOKOUT MOUNTAIN

Many of Chattanooga's most famous attractions are on Lookout Mountain, located south of downtown. The best way to get to Lookout Mountain from the city is by driving south on Broad Street. After about two miles, Broad splits into the Ochs Highway (Route 58) and the Cummings Highway (Highways 42, 72, 11, and 64). Follow Ochs to get to the base of the Incline Railroad or Rock City; follow Cummings to get to Point Park and Ruby Falls. Both roads take you to Lookout Mountain.

You can also get to Lookout Mountain by parking at the bottom and riding the Incline

Railroad. When you reach the top, you can walk to Point Park. Other attractions are beyond walking distance, however.

Whenever you are driving on Lookout Mountain, do it with caution. The roads are narrow, windy, heavily trafficked, and—in some places—precarious. Drive slowly and carefully (seriously, no texting!).

SIGHTS
◖ Tennessee Aquarium

The Tennessee Aquarium (1 Broad St., 800/262-0695, www.tnaqua.org, daily 10 A.M.–6 P.M., adults $24.95, children 3–12 $14.95) is Chattanooga's landmark attraction. Two huge buildings with angular glass roofs house Ocean Journey and River Journey, salt- and freshwater aquariums with more than 12,000 animals in all. It has a more educational bent than facilities like Atlanta's Georgia Aquarium, which is more entertainment focused. Built in 1992, the aquarium was the first act in Chattanooga's remarkable comeback as a city.

Ocean Journey showcases saltwater creatures, including sharks, rays, and colorful coral reef fish. River Journey follows the watershed from an Appalachian cove forest to a humid delta swamp and includes exhibits on the major rivers of the world, including the Tennessee, which is literally right out front. Standout exhibits include the playful river otters, the boneless beauties—jellyfish, octopus, and cuttlefish—and the American alligator. In between these, there are literally hundreds of captivating and high-quality exhibits of all types of water creatures. The music you hear is designed to reflect the music you'd hear in the region of the world where you'd find the fish you see. On some days you may even experience live music, such as a bluegrass fiddler in the delta exhibit.

Outside the aquarium there are fountains and a wading pool. Or you can walk over the riverfront and look out at the mighty Tennessee. In addition to the aquarium itself, there is an

sandbar shark at the Tennessee Aquarium

IMAX 3-D Theater, which shows nature-related films daily. Tickets may be purchased separately (adults $9.95, children $8.50) or as part of a discounted admission package with the aquarium.

The aquarium can get crowded on weekends, as well as on weekdays in summer. Start out early to avoid the worst crowds, and remember that your admission ticket is good all day, so you can take a midday break for lunch and return.

Other Downtown Sights

Chattanooga's African American history is preserved at the **Bessie Smith Hall and Chattanooga African American Museum** (200 E. Martin Luther King Blvd., 423/266-8658, www.bessiesmithcc.org, Mon.–Fri. 10 A.M.–5 P.M., Sat. noon–4 P.M., adults $7, seniors and students $5, children 6–12 $3). The museum is located at the site of the Martin Hotel, once a popular African American hotel and restaurant. There are hundreds of photographs of black Chattanoogans, with panels that describe the African American community's contributions in sports, the arts, business, government, and culture. There are pictures of famous black Chattanoogans including Bessie Smith, Samuel L. Jackson, Valaida Smith, and Roland Hayes. The exhibits include information about African culture, accomplishments, and art.

Just down the hall, in the lobby of the Bessie Smith Hall, is an exhibit dedicated to the legendary blues singer. Smith grew up poor in Chattanooga, having been orphaned at age nine. She developed her singing talent performing for pennies on the streets of Chattanooga. Smith was discovered by Ma Rainey and, later, Columbia Records, and for a period in the 1920s she was the highest-paid American black woman in the entertainment world.

Smith's success did not last. After a bad marriage and personal problems including alcohol abuse, Smith was in the early stages of a comeback when she died in a car accident in north Mississippi in 1937. She was buried in an unmarked grave in Philadelphia. In 1970, rock singer Janis Joplin found out about the grave and bought a headstone, which reads "The greatest blues singer in the world will never stop singing."

Inside the hall you will see photographs of Smith, old concert posters, and a dress she wore in the early days of her singing career.

The **International Towing and Recovery Hall of Fame and Museum** (3315 Broad St., 423/267-3132, www.internationaltowingmuseum.org, Mar.–Oct. Mon.–Sat. 9 A.M.–5 P.M., Nov.–Feb. Mon.–Sat. 10 A.M.–4:30 P.M., year-round Sun. 11 A.M.–5 P.M., adults $8, seniors $7, children 6–18 $4) showcases antique and modern tow trucks and other recovery vehicles. The museum is located in Chattanooga because the first tow truck was fabricated nearby at the Ernest Holmes Company. The museum's hall of fame memorializes people who have made significant contributions to the towing and recovery industry. The Wall of the Fallen remembers operators who lost their lives on the job.

The **Chattanooga Discovery Museum** (321 Chestnut St., 423/756-2738, www.cdmfun.org, Mon.–Sat. 10 A.M.–5 P.M., extended summer hours 9:30 A.M.–5:30 P.M., Sun. noon–5 P.M., closed on Wed. Sept.–Feb., $11.95, discounts with your aquarium ticket stub) is a hands-on museum specifically designed for children under 12. Activities include RiverPlay, where kids can pilot a riverboat, and an archaeological dig area, plus a regularly rotating collection of temporary exhibitions. There is a special play area for toddlers, too.

The **Chattanooga History Center** (2 Broad St., 423/265-3247, www.chattanoogahistory.com, Mon.–Fri. 9 A.M.–5 P.M.) closed its location at 400 Chestnut Street in 2007. The museum is developing its new facility, and the exhibits are still in the works. Even so, the center is worth a visit. The center also leads themed tours around the city, including several Civil War tours. Fees vary based on tour. Custom tours can also be arranged.

The **Chattanooga Zoo** (Warner Park, 1254 E. 3rd St., 423/697-1322, www.chattzoo.org, daily 9 A.M.–5 P.M., adults $8.95, seniors $6.95, children 3–12 $5.95, children 2 and under free) is a modest yet fun animal park. The six-acre facility located inside Warner Park houses chimpanzees, red pandas, snow leopards, spider moneys, and jaguars, among others. There is also a petting zoo. A $4.2 million front entrance to the zoo from Holtzclaw Avenue (Warner Park) was constructed in 2008; this makes it easier to see and find the zoo. The zoo celebrated its 75th anniversary in 2012. The zoo is not in walking distance of the main downtown attractions.

Bluff View

The bluff overlooking the Tennessee River and downtown Chattanooga is the city's arts center. The foremost attraction here is the **Hunter Museum of American Art** (10 Bluff View, 423/267-0968, www.huntermuseum.org, Mon.–Tues., Fri.–Sat. 10 A.M.–5 P.M., Wed. and Sun. noon–5 P.M., Thurs. 8 A.M.–8 P.M., adults $9.95, children 3–17 $4.95, children under 13 free holidays and weekends). Housed in the former home of Coca-Cola magnate and philanthropist George Thomas Hunter, the Hunter Museum has one of the most important collections of American art in the Southeast. The permanent collection includes works from the Hudson River School, American Impressionism, Ashcan School, Regionalist, Early Modern, and Contemporary movements. Major touring exhibits are also on display, and visitors enjoy dramatic views of the river below.

On a pleasant day, stroll through the **Bluff View Art District Sculpture Garden,** affiliated with the Hunter Museum but open to the public at no charge.

The **Houston Museum of the Decorative Arts** (201 High St., 423/267-7176, Mon.–Fri. 9:30 A.M.–4 P.M., Sat. noon–4 P.M., adults $8, children 4–17 $3.50) houses the decorative arts collection of Anna Safley Houston. Houston was a colorful character who died in relative poverty in 1951, having refused to sell any part of her valuable collection of porcelain and glassware.

Inside the museum you will find parts of Houston's remarkable collection, including antique money banks, steins, face mugs, miniature lamps, and glass baskets, as well as early American furniture and coverlets.

Main Street

South of downtown, at the corner of Main and Market Streets, is the legendary **Chattanooga Choo Choo** (1400 Market St., 423/266-5000, www.choochoo.com), a railroad car. The Choo Choo is located inside the city's old Terminal Station, which is now a hotel. The terminal was built in 1909 to accommodate the increasing number of passengers who arrived in the city aboard trains including the Chattanooga Choo Choo, which ran from Cincinnati, Ohio, to Chattanooga starting in 1880. The train was made famous in a song by Harry Warren and Mack Gordon, performed in the late 1940s by the Glenn Miller Orchestra. The tune starts with the lines: "Pardon me, boy, Is that that Chattanooga Choo Choo?" It is impossible to stand here and not have that refrain pass through your head.

The main sight here is an old wood-burning engine, which is similar to what would have powered the famous Choo Choo. The engine you see actually came from the Smoky Mountain Railroad, which ran between Knoxville and the Smokies in the 1940s.

There are shops, restaurants, and a small garden around the old railroad engine. Children will enjoy the **Model Railroad Museum** (1400 Market St., 423/266-5000, Mon.–Thurs. 3–7 P.M., Fri.–Sun. 10 A.M.–7 P.M., adults $4, children 3–17 $2), a miniature world with 3,000 feet of model railroad track, 120 locomotives, and 80 passenger cars.

Better than the Choo Choo, however, is Chattanooga's real, working railroad. The **Tennessee Valley Railroad** (4119 Cromwell Rd., 423/894-8028, www.tvrail.com, adults $16, children $10) offers railroad excursions departing from Grand Junction Station on the other side of Chickamauga Creek and Missionary Ridge. The hour-long ride covers six miles, travels through the Missionary Ridge railroad tunnel, and includes a stop at the East Chattanooga repair shop and turntable. The Missionary Ridge Local, as the excursion is named, leaves several times per day, depending on the time of year.

The railroad also offers occasional trips to other destinations in Tennessee and north Georgia.

C Lookout Mountain

Lookout Mountain is part of the Cumberland Plateau. It extends 83 miles through Tennessee, Alabama, and Georgia, but the northernmost tip, which overlooks Chattanooga, is its most famous part. No journey to the city is complete without taking a drive up the mountain to enjoy exceptional views and some of the most iconic of Tennessee attractions.

Point Park (1110 E. Brow Rd., adults $3, children 15 and under free) offers the best views off Lookout Mountain. This park is maintained by the National Park Service as part of the Chickamauga and Chattanooga National Military Park, and there is a **visitors center** (423/821-7786, daily 8:30 A.M.–5 P.M.) at the gates of the park. The best thing about the park, however, are the views of the Cumberland Plateau, Chattanooga, and the Cherokee National Forest in the eastward distance. The Tennessee River winds languidly through the landscape. On a clear day, it is stunning.

Students of the Civil War should visit the **Battles for Chattanooga Electric Map and Museum** (1110 E. Brow Rd., 423/821-2812, www.battlesforchattanooga.com, daily 10 A.M.–5 P.M., summer 9 A.M.–6 P.M., adults $8, children 3–12 $6), a private museum that

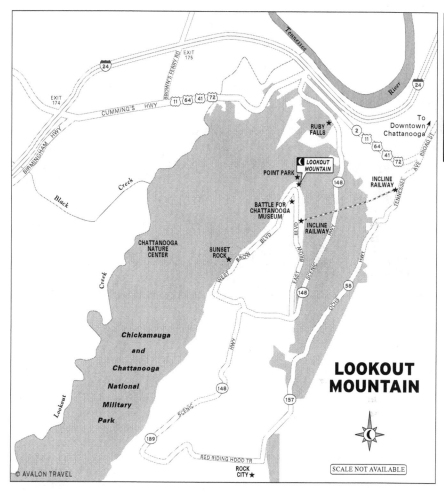

chronicles several Civil War battles, including the Battle Above the Clouds on Lookout Mountain, that took place in the area. An electric map, which shows 5,000 miniature soldiers and hundreds of lights, is a showpiece of the museum. Don't miss the gift shop if you are a collector of things relating to Civil War history. The museum is located next door to Point Park.

Chattanooga's most famous attraction may well be **Rock City** (1400 Patten Rd., 800/854-0675, www.seerockcity.com, Jan.–Mar. 10 and Nov. 4–15 daily 8:30 A.M.–5 P.M., Mar. 11–May 25 and Sept. 4–Nov. 3 daily 8:30 A.M.–6 P.M., May 26–Sept. 3 daily 8:30 A.M.–8 P.M., Nov. 16–Jan. 5 daily 8:30 A.M.–4 P.M., adults $18.95, children 3–12 $10.95, package discounts available if you buy the tickets in combination with Lookout Mountain attractions). A remarkable, yet hokey, rock garden with exceptional views, including one that encompasses seven states, Rock City was one of the first tourist attractions in the area, opening in 1932. The

© LIZ LITTMAN

From Rock City you can see seven states.

See Rock City billboards painted on barns throughout the South were legendary and iconic; today the gift shop at Rock City overflows with related mementos, including birdhouses with the message painted on them.

Visitors to Rock City travel a 4,100-foot "Enchanted Trail" that winds through ancient rock formations, including a 90-foot waterfall, narrow walkways, and a 1,000-ton balancing rock. Lover's Leap is the viewpoint from which you can see, on a clear day, Georgia, Tennessee, Alabama, North Carolina, South Carolina, Virginia, and Kentucky. Fairyland Caverns and Mother Goose Village are underground collections of quirky folk art (illuminated by black light). The 180-foot swinging bridge over the open air is memorable, as are the gardens of perennials and native plants. Unlike most botanic gardens, Rock City welcomes dogs. More than half a million people check out Rock City every year, but the parking lots and trails are well designed to handle crowds.

Ruby Falls (1720 S. Scenic Hwy., 800/755-7105, www.rubyfalls.com, daily 8 A.M.–8 P.M., adults $17.95, children 3–12 $9.95, although there are package discounts if you buy the tickets in combination with other Lookout Mountain attractions) is an underground waterfall located deep within Lookout Mountain (in fact, it claims to the be tallest underground waterfall in the country). The traditional entrance to Lookout Mountain Cave was closed in 1905 when the Southern Railway Company sealed it during the construction of a railroad along the side of the mountain. Chemist and entrepreneur Leo Lambert had explored the cave before and believed it would be a lucrative tourist attraction. So in 1928 he started to bore an elevator shaft down into the mountain to the cave. Lambert's unusual plan worked, and by 1930 visitors were touring the cave and the 145-foot waterfall, which Lambert named not for a color, but for his wife, Ruby.

The entrance to Ruby Falls is in a massive

© R&R MARKETING

Take in the view from Lookout Mountain Incline Railway.

daily 9 A.M.–6 P.M., June–Aug. daily 8:30 A.M.–9:30 P.M., Nov.–Mar. daily 10 A.M.–6 P.M., adults $14, children 3–12 $7, although there are package discounts if you buy the tickets in combination with other Lookout Mountain attractions), which climbs from Chattanooga to the top of Lookout Mountain. The railway was built in 1895 and has been ferrying visitors up the mountain ever since.

It takes about 10 minutes to make the journey from the bottom of the mountain to the top, where there are gift shops and restaurants. Point Park is a short walk away, but other Lookout Mountain attractions require a car. Parking is free at the bottom of the mountain, but a fee is charged to park at the top.

On the western edge of Lookout Mountain, in the midst of the upscale residential neighborhood, is **Sunset Rock.** A natural landmark admired for generations, this sheer bluff looks westward, and the view at sunset is indeed spectacular. It draws rock climbers who rappel down the sheer face of the bluff. The short hike (0.2 mile) down to the rock is steep and rough; wear comfortable shoes and take your time. There is no wall or fence blocking the sheer drop down the face of the rock (which makes for much better pictures).

Nestled on Lookout Mountain are 317 acres of the **Chattanooga Arboretum and Nature Center** (400 Garden Rd., 423/821-1160, www.chattanooganaturecenter.org, Mon.–Sat. 9 A.M.–5 P.M., Sun. (summer only) 1–5 P.M., adults $8, seniors and children 4–11 $5). This is a park, nature preserve, and environmental education facility. Visitors have the opportunity to see 30 different native animal species, including red wolves, bald eagles, bobcats, and raccoons, in the Wildlife Wanderland. There is also a 1,400-foot boardwalk that meanders through a seasonal wetland and lowland forest, and takes you to the George S. Bryan Tree House. Gardens include a fragrance garden and organic community garden, and there is a bird

limestone building modeled after an Irish castle. It was built out of stone brought up while Lambert was drilling the elevator shaft through the mountain; the top floor was added in 1976.

The tour of Ruby Falls takes about 1.5 hours in total and involves walking a bit less than a mile on paved underground paths. Your tour guide will tell the standard kitschy jokes, and the lighting on many of the rock formations feel forced. But when you get to the spot where Ruby Falls' waters thunder 145 feet to the pool beneath, it is hard not to be impressed. The tour guide will turn off the lights and then turn on the ruby-tinted bulbs, and you'll get the chance to hear and see the falls close up, if you choose.

Much of the power that now illuminates the Ruby Falls complex is generated by green energy options.

The steepest passenger train in the world is the **Incline Railway** (3917 St. Elmo Ave. and 827 E. Brow Rd., 423/821-4224, www.ride-theincline.com, Apr.–May and Sept.–Oct.

and butterfly café. In addition, there are miles of trails for hiking or biking in the adjoining Reflection Riding Arboretum and Botanical Garden. Come on a pleasant day and plan on spending several hours exploring the nature center. As is the case at many nature centers, dogs are not permitted.

Signal Mountain

Signal Mountain perches on the top of Walden's Ridge about 15 minutes' drive north of Chattanooga. Named because it is believed the Cherokee used it for signal fires, Signal Mountain later evolved into an upscale residential community. The Signal Mountain Inn once was a popular tourist destination; today it is a retirement home.

Visitors should make the challenging uphill drive to visit **Signal Point** (Signal Point Rd., 423/821-7786), a park that offers a dramatic view of the Tennessee River below. The site, managed by the National Park Service, is part of the Chickamauga and Chattanooga National Military Park and was an important vantage point during the Civil War. It is the southern terminus of the 300-plus-mile Cumberland Trail.

To get to Signal Mountain, take Highway 127 to Mountain Creek Road.

ENTERTAINMENT AND EVENTS
The Arts

Chattanooga has made significant investment in its arts offerings during the last decade, and it shows. Programs like CreateHere (www.createhere.org) helped develop loans for individual artists to encourage them to buy property in the Main Street/Southside District, and that had the intended effect of attracting more artists of all stripes to the city.

The **Allied Arts Alliance of Greater Chattanooga** (406 Frazier Ave., 423/756-2787, www.alliedartschattanooga.org, Mon.–Fri. 8:30 A.M.–5 P.M.) is an umbrella organization that promotes the arts. Contact them for an arts guide to the city or for information about upcoming events.

Chattanooga's **Arts and Education Council** (3069 Broad St., 423/267-1218, www.artsedcouncil.org) organizes a variety of programs, including film festivals and literary conferences.

VENUES

The jewel of Chattanooga's arts venues is the **Tivoli Theater** (709 Broad St., 423/757-5050), a beaux arts–style performance hall that has been restored and equipped with modern amenities. Built in 1921, the Tivoli played films and live dramas to sold-out Chattanooga audiences through the 1950s. But with the advent of television, shopping malls, and the automobile, the downtown theater declined and narrowly escaped demolition in 1961.

After years of consideration and fundraising, the Tivoli was totally restored in the late 1980s and reopened to adoring crowds in 1989. Its domed ceiling, crystal chandeliers, and ornate finishes make this a lovely venue. There's typically free parking for ticketholders at the BlueCross/BlueShield of Tennessee garage.

Chattanooga's **Memorial Auditorium** (399 McCallie Ave., 423/642-8497) is another popular venue for concerts, performances, and special events. Built in 1924 as a memorial to the soldiers and sailors of World War I, Memorial Auditorium was then the largest space in Chattanooga for concerts other events. It housed boxing matches, roller derbies, tennis matches, banquets, and religious revivals.

VISUAL ARTS

Once a forgotten part of the city, the **Southside** neighborhood (http://southsidechattanooga.org), which largely is made up of Main Street, is a collection of former industrial buildings that have been repurposed as artist studios, galleries, boutiques, and more. On the last Friday of every month 5–8 P.M. is the art stroll here,

The Tivoli Theater has been a sign of entertainment in Chattanooga for more than 85 years.

when galleries are open late and artists are on hand to talk about their new works, but any day is a good day to walk by and gaze at the creativity on display in these windows.

The work of local and regional artists is featured at the **Association for Visual Artists Gallery** (30 Frazier Ave., 423/265-4282, www. avartists.org, Tues.–Sat. 11 A.M.–5 P.M.), located on Chattanooga's North Shore.

The **River Gallery** (400 E. 2nd St., 423/265-5033, www.river-gallery.com, Mon.–Sat. 10 A.M.–5 P.M., Sun. 1–5 P.M.) is located in a turn-of-the-20th-century home in the Bluff View Arts District. It exhibits fine arts and crafts from local, regional, and international artists.

MUSIC AND DANCE

The **Chattanooga Symphony & Opera** (701 Broad St., 423/267-8583, www.chattanoogasymphony. org) performs classical, opera, pops, and family concerts every year at the Tivoli Theater.

Ballet Tennessee (3202 Kelly's Ferry Rd., 423/821-2055, www.ballettennessee.org) is Chattanooga's foremost ballet company and school. They perform at the Tivoli Theater and Memorial Auditorium.

Track29 (1400 Market St., 423/521-2929), named for its location at the historic Chattanooga Choo Choo, is the city's hippest concert venue. Shows are booked by the same folks who pull together Bonnaroo, so they get access to a diverse cross section of acts.

THEATER

The **Chattanooga Theatre Centre** (400 River Rd., 423/267-8534, www.theatrecentre.com) is a community theater that produces musicals, comedies, and dramas.

CINEMAS

The **Independent Film Series** (www.artsedcouncil.org) brings award-winning independent films to Chattanooga's downtown Bijou Theatre two times per year. The **Back Row Film Series** (www.backrowfilms.com) takes place at the Hunter Museum and features film screenings followed by a related guest speaker.

Festivals and Events
SPRING

Billed as a writer's conference for readers, the biennial **Conference on Southern Literature** (www.southernlitconference.org) brings heavyweights in Southern literature to Chattanooga for three days of lectures, discussions, and readings in March. On off years, the Arts and Education Council hosts the **Chattanooga Festival of Writers,** a celebration of the craft of writing.

In April the **4 Bridges Arts Festival** (www.4bridgesartsfestival.org) brings 150 artists (chosen from more than 700 applicants) to the First Tennessee Pavilion downtown for two days of exhibits, children's activities, and acoustic music. It is a good opportunity to purchase original artwork in a wide variety of formats or just people-watch (in 2011, more than 18,000 people attended). There is typically a modest admission fee.

In May, the Chattanooga Bicycle Club and Outdoor Chattanooga host **3 States, 3 Mountains** (www.chattbike.com), a 100-mile bicycle race that originates and ends at Finley Stadium in downtown Chattanooga. There are also options for 88-, 62- and 25-mile courses.

SUMMER

One of Chattanooga's largest annual events is the **Riverbend Festival** (www.riverbendfestival.com). Taking place in mid-June, the festival stretches for one mile along the city's waterfront and features multiple stages with jazz, blues, rock, pop, country, folk, and classical performers. The festival also includes the Bessie Smith Strut, a street festival along Martin Luther King Boulevard.

On Fridays May–August, **Rhythm and Noon** provides free midday concerts at Miller Plaza downtown. Performers play classical, folk, rock, jazz, swing, choral music, and blues. The concerts are a warm-up for **Nightfall** (http://nightfallchattanooga.com), free Friday-evening concerts held at Miller Plaza Memorial Day– the last weekend in September. Each concert starts out with a local act and concludes with a headliner. The schedule includes a wide range of genres, from world music to bluegrass.

FALL

On the Friday night of Labor Day weekend, kick off your shoes at **SwingFest** (www.downtownchattanooga.org), an open-air concert featuring local and regional big-band performers.

Every September, Chattanooga's **Culture Fest** (www.artsedcouncil.org) turns Coolidge Park into a festival of diverse cultures. International performers, foods from around the world, a merchandise bazaar, and unique arts and crafts are a few of the attractions.

Bluegrass music comes to the waterfront with the **Three Sisters Festival** (www.3sistersbluegrass.com), a three-day festival held in early October at Ross's Landing. Three Sisters is held in conjunction with **RiverRocks Chattanooga** (www.riverrockschattanooga.com), a nine-day celebration of all things outdoor. There are more than 90 events at RiverRocks, including stand-up paddling races, hot-air balloon rides, cycling, biking, and running events, plus live music, kids' activities, and funky demonstrations.

WINTER

Each November brings the **Head of the Hooch Regatta** (www.headofthehooch.org), the second-largest regatta in the country, to Chattanooga.

SHOPPING
Malls

Hamilton Place (2100 Hamilton Place Blvd., 423/894-7177, www.hamiltonplace.com) is Chattanooga's foremost place for shopping. Located at exit 4A off I-75 northeast of downtown, Hamilton Place has more than 150 stores, including JCPenney, Sears, Dillard's, and Belk.

Books

Chattanooga's best downtown bookstore is **Winder Binder** (40 Frazier Ave., 423/413-8999, www.winderbinder.com), which is also an art gallery and hipster hangout.

RECREATION
Parks

In many ways, Chattanooga, with countless ways to get out and enjoy nature, is like one big park. It seems like there are as many boat access spots along the banks of the river as there are parking lots.

Two of the best city parks are located on the banks of the Tennessee River. **Ross's Landing Park and Plaza,** adjacent to the Tennessee Aquarium at the end of Broad

Street, is a sculpted park that uses concrete, glass, stone, and grass to depict the timeline of Chattanooga's history. It is a nice place to stroll, people-watch, or enjoy a picnic.

On the other side of the river, **Coolidge Park** is even nicer. This grassy park has paths for walking, benches for sitting, and a glass-enclosed carousel to entertain children and adults. A ride on the old-style merry-go-round is just $0.50. Come here for lovely views of Chattanooga's downtown.

Outside of town, **Booker T. Washington State Park** (5801 Champion Rd., 423/894-4955) is a day-use park located off Highway 58, on the northeast side of town, whose primary attraction is Lake Chickamauga. There are several boat launching ramps. Waterskiing, fishing, stand-up paddling, kayaking, and pleasure cruising are popular activities. There are also picnic facilities and an Olympic-size swimming pool.

Farther outside of town, **Harrison Bay State Park** (8411 Harrison Bay Rd., Harrison, 423/344-6214) is also located on Lake Chickamauga. It is named for part of the lake, Harrison Bay, that covers what was once the last Cherokee Indian settlement in this area. The land was inundated in 1940 with the construction and closure of the Chickamauga Dam by the Tennessee Valley Authority.

There are public boat ramps, and all types of boats are allowed. In addition, there are picnic facilities, an Olympic-size pool, and a campground with RV and tent sites. There are also six miles of hiking trails and a bike path.

Biking

Bicycling is a required mode of transport for Chattanoogans. With bike-to-work programs and an innovative 300-bike fleet initiative, Chattanooga is well ahead of the curve when it comes to promoting alternative ways of getting around town.

There are bike lanes on many downtown streets, as well as bike-friendly trails along the Chattanooga waterfront, at the Chickamauga Dam, and at the TVA's Raccoon Mountain Reservoir, making the area accessible on two wheels for both visitors and locals.

Bike Chattanooga (www.bikechattanooga.org) provides safety courses for bikers, promotes bike riding, and publishes information about recreational bike riding in the area, as well as details on the new public bike sharing program. The **Chattanooga Bicycle Club** (www.chattbike.com) is another good option for local biking info.

For rentals and other bike-gear needs, try **Trek Bicycle Store of Chattanooga** (307 Manufacturers Rd., 423/648-2100, http://trekstorechattanooga.com), **River City Bicycles** (122 Tremont St., 423/265-7176, http://rivercitybikes.com), or **Suck Creek Cycle** (501 Cherokee Blvd., 423/266-8883, http://suckcreek.com).

River Cruises

When visiting a city built on the river, you might as well take advantage and get *on* the river. **Blue Moon Cruises** (888/993-2583, www.bluemooncruises.org, $40) offers seasonal cruises down the Tennessee River aboard a 70-foot Skipperliner cruise boat. Blue Moon's cruise down the Tennessee River Gorge lasts about 3.5 hours and departs morning and afternoon from the Chattanooga Pier, off Ross's Landing waterfront park. The naturalist-led ecocruise emphasizes the animals and plants you see on the riverbanks, as well as the cultural and historical significance of the river over the years. There are also seasonal fall color cruises and other specialty tours.

Spectator Sports

The **Chattanooga Lookouts** (201 Power Alley, 423/267-2208, box office 423/267-4849, www.lookouts.com, general admission adults $4, children $2, box seats $6–8), a farm team for the Cincinnati Reds, play at AT&T Field downtown. The baseball season runs April–September.

Amusement Parks

Just over the state line in Georgia is **Lake Winnepesaukah** (1730 Lakeview Dr., Rossville GA, 706/866-5681, www.lakewinnie.com, Apr.–Sept. Wed.–Thurs. 10 A.M.–8 P.M., Fri.–Sat. 10 A.M.–10 P.M., Sun. noon–10 P.M., unlimited rides pass adults $26, seniors and children $10), a family-oriented amusement park operating since 1925. The Cannon Ball is a wooden roller coaster, and the Boat Chute is the oldest mill chute ride in the United States. There are also modern rides, including the Oh-Zone and Wild Lightning. In addition to rides, Lake Winnepesaukah has a midway and food vendors. In addition to the unlimited pass, tickets to rides can be purchased individually.

To find Lake Winnepesaukah, drive south on I-75 to the Route 41 exit. Drive on Ringold Road for two miles to McBrien Road. Turn left, and the park is two miles ahead on Lakeview Drive.

Hang Gliding

The mountains around Chattanooga are ideal for hang gliding. The **Lookout Mountain Flight Park** (7201 Scenic Hwy., Rising Fawn GA, 706/398-3541, www.hanglide.com, daily 9 A.M.–6 P.M., closed Wed.) offers tandem glides with a certified instructor and lessons appropriate for all levels. The flight school is the largest hang gliding school in America. A single tandem flight, which lasts about 15 minutes, is $149. A daylong package that includes a tandem flight plus five "bunny hill" low-altitude flights is $199.

Paddling

Whether it is in a kayak, canoe, or on a stand-up paddleboard, Chattanoogans love to get on the local waters, both flat water and white water. Rent boards from **SUP Paddleboard** (900 Dallas Rd., 423/421-1403, www.suppaddleboard.com) or **L2 Boards** (First and Market Sts., 423/531-7873, www.l2boards.com). For canoes, try **Chattanooga Nature Center** (400 Garden Rd., 423/821-1160, www.chattanooganaturecenter.org). **OutVenture Kayak** (5051 Gann Store Rd., 423/842-6629) offers guided kayak trips all over the area, including a downtown kayak trip.

ACCOMMODATIONS
Under $100

Interstate motels offer good value in the Chattanooga area. In this category, the **Econo Lodge Lookout Mountain** (150 Browns Ferry Rd., 423/821-9000, $65–85) is a good choice for its location convenient to downtown and Lookout Mountain, and for its clean rooms and amenities, including in-room microwaves, refrigerators, free wireless, and coffeemakers. Guests also enjoy a free continental breakfast. There's an outdoor pool open in the summer.

$100-150

❰ **Bluff View Inn** (Bluff View Art District, 423/265-5033, ext. 2, www.bluffviewartdistrict.com, $105–240) consists of 16 rooms in three different historic properties located in the peaceful Bluff View Art District. Guest rooms in the Maclellen House, Martin House, and Thompson House range from modest-size quarters with a shower-tub combination to luxurious suites with river views, private balconies, and sitting rooms. A full sit-down breakfast is included in room rates and is served at the Back Inn Café.

If you thought it was a new idea to turn an outmoded train station into a hotel, think again. The Chattanooga Station stopped operating as a train station in 1970, and just three years later it reopened as a tourist attraction. Nineteen years later it was retooled again, this time into the hotel that you see today. The **Chattanooga Choo Choo Holiday Inn** (1400 Market St., 800/872-2529, www.choochoo.com, $120–190) consists of three buildings of hotel rooms, plus distinctive train-car accommodations. The hotel rooms are clean and generous in size, although not particularly modern or charming;

Today, the old Chattanooga Choo Choo train station is a magnificent hotel lobby.

they feature amenities such as wireless Internet, in-room coffeemakers, and king-size beds.

But what makes the Choo Choo special is its railcar accommodations. These old sleeper cars have been converted into hotel-style rooms with four-poster beds, desks, and private bathrooms. Each room has a queen-size bed, and some feature pull-out trundle beds ideal for family accommodations, although all are very small (because they used to be sleeper cars). The lobby is the most interesting feature of the hotel.

In addition to hotel rooms, the Choo Choo has three different restaurants, an ice cream shop, retail shops, and a railway museum. The lobby and upscale restaurant located in the atrium of the old train station lobby are dramatic and beautiful.

The **Stone Fort Inn** (120 E. 10th St., 423/267-7866, www.stonefortinn.com, $120–190) is an old-fashioned city hotel with a modern, chic feel. Located about 10 blocks from the aquarium and close to federal and state office buildings, the Stone Fort Inn has 20 guest rooms of varying sizes. All rooms have high-speed Internet connections, oversized whirlpool tubs, luxury bath soaps, claw-foot soaking tubs, TV/VCRs, and cheerful decor. Polished terrazzo floors, marble fireplaces, well-stocked bookshelves, an 1885 grand piano, and a 1920s slate pool table all conjure an atmosphere of cozy elegance in this circa-1909 hotel building. On weekdays there is a continental breakfast and on weekends a gourmet sit-down morning meal. The dining area becomes a public café and restaurant on Wednesday and Thursday evenings, with inviting selections from the bar, live acoustic music, and a menu of inventive small plates. Children under 12 are not permitted at the Old Stone Fort, unless you rent the whole hotel for a special event.

The Chattanoogan (1201 S. Broad St., 423/756-3400, www.chattanooganhotel.com, $119–159) is an upscale hotel and conference center located just south of downtown. The hotel offers 199 guest rooms and suites, many of them with views of Lookout Mountain, and all appointed with modern furnishings, fabrics, and amenities. A dramatic see-through glass fireplace in the lobby is a talking point and attraction in its own right. An on-site spa, conference center, and three restaurants round out the resort's amenities. The Chattanoogan opened in 2001 and underwent extensive renovation in 2007 to keep the decor current and comfortable.

$150-200

Mayor's Mansion Inn (801 Vine St., 423/265-5000, www.mayorsmansioninn.com, $160–295) is a luxury bed-and-breakfast located in an 1889 Victorian mansion built for the mayor of Chattanooga. Mayor's Mansion has 11 guest rooms and is located in the Fort Wood District near the University of Tennessee, less than one mile from downtown Chattanooga. Each guest room is unique, with distinctive fabrics, wallpaper, and antique furniture. Guests may feel like they are bedding down in a home that could just as easily be open for tours. Common areas include a stone terrace, verandahs, and a library. Elegant indulgences include nightly turn-down service, a three-course breakfast, and soft cotton robes. Guests may also take advantage of concierge service, Internet access, and other amenities like ironing boards and a video library.

Another longtime favorite downtown hotel is the **Sheraton Read House Hotel** (827 Broad St., 800/691-1255, $115–290). Located in a historic redbrick Georgian-style building near the theater district, and about 10 blocks from the aquarium, the Sheraton offers its guests luxury and comfort. Its 219 guest rooms and suites include high-speed Internet, Drexel Heritage furniture, and luxurious beds. There is an indoor zero-edge pool with a waterfall, top-notch workout room, on-site steak house, and

The historic Sheraton Read House Hotel has a great location in downtown Chattanooga.

© TODD EVANS

Starbucks coffee shop. It is a short walk to the riverfront attractions.

Camping

Harrison Bay State Park (8411 Harrison Bay Rd., Harrison, 423/344-7966), located about 20 minutes drive from downtown, has 134 RV sites and 28 tent-only sites in its lakefront campground. Rates are $12–18.50. No reservations are accepted; Tennessee State Parks are first come, first served.

FOOD
Downtown

For good food, casual-yet-polished service, and a convivial atmosphere, go where many Chattanoogans go for a meal out. **212 Market** (212 Market St., 423/265-1212, daily 11 A.M.–3 P.M., Mon.–Thurs. 5–9:30 P.M., Fri.–Sat. 5–10 P.M., Sun. 5–9 P.M., lunch $7–14, dinner $15–30) serves upscale daily lunch and dinner specials like ginger-glazed salmon, wild mushroom ravioli, and Carolina mountain trout. The 212 Pecan Chicken Club is a delectable lunchtime favorite. This was one of the first downtown restaurants to open following the area's rebirth in the early 1990s, and it is still a first choice for dining in the city.

When you give an old-fashioned diner a makeover, the result is **The Blue Plate** (191 Chestnut St., Unit B, 423/648-6767, Mon.–Thurs. 11 A.M.–9 P.M., Fri. 11 A.M.–10 P.M., Sat. 9 A.M.–10 P.M., Sun. 9 A.M.–9 P.M., $6–18), a downtown eatery with sleek lines, fresh food, and a home-style heart. You can order breakfast eggs and pancakes all day, or choose a plump, juicy burger. The chef salad is piled high with pulled chicken, diced eggs, and mixed cheeses, and the entrées include fried-to-order chicken and not your mother's baked meat loaf. Don't skip the green beans. Or the Moon Pie cheesecake. To prove that this is not your everyday lunch counter, you can also order from a full bar, although the spot is perfectly kid friendly.

Tucked away in the downtown business district is Chattanooga's favorite vegetarian eatery, albeit only open for lunch. The **Country Life Vegetarian Restaurant** (809 Market St., 423/634-9925, Mon.–Thurs. 11:30 A.M.–2:30 P.M., $5–10) serves whole-grain, homegrown, all-vegetarian food. The specials change daily and include things like tofu and brown rice, butternut squash quiche, and veggie fajitas. There is also a well-stocked salad bar.

You might be surprised how good England tastes in Chattanooga. The **English Rose Tearoom** (1401 Market St., 423/265-5900, Tues.–Sun. 11 A.M.–5 P.M., $5–15) serves authentic British Isles fare, including finger sandwiches, ploughman's lunch, and cottage pie. Come into this welcoming spot for an afternoon tea with scones and sandwiches, or for a meal of steak pies, Dover sole, flounder, or Cornish pasties. The atmosphere is on the refined side, but it's not uptight. The English Rose offers a nice change of pace.

Upscale Southern comfort food is the draw at **Mt. Vernon Restaurant** (3535 Broad St., 423/266-6591, www.mymtvernon.com, Mon.–Thurs. 11 A.M.–9 P.M., Fri. 11 A.M.–9:30 P.M., Sat. 4–9:30 P.M., $9–16). Located near the base of Lookout Mountain, Mt. Vernon is a favorite among Chattanoogans, who come for its familiar food, generous portions, and hometown feel. Specialties include Southern fried chicken ($13) and Maryland crab cakes ($17). The fried green tomatoes appetizer is always a favorite. At lunchtime you can also order from the under-$10 sandwich menu, with choices like BLT, grouper sandwich, and the Mt. Vernon Club.

Chattanooga's best meat-and-three diner is **Zarzour's Café** (1627 Rossville Ave., 423/266-0424, Mon.–Fri. 11 A.M.–2 P.M., $5–8), a hole-in-the-wall tucked away in the wrong part of town. Zarzour's was founded by Lebanese immigrant Charles Zarzour in 1913, and the eatery has persisted through good times and bad for the past nine-plus decades under the family's ownership. But it is not Middle Eastern specialties that bring in the regulars; it is some of the best home-cooked Southern food in the city. Flavorful turnip greens, creamy potatoes, comforting baked spaghetti, and hot-from-the-skillet corn bread are among the dishes on the menu. Each day you can choose from one of three main-dish entrées, accompanied by your choice of two side dishes. Or order a hand-patted burger from the grill. This is a cash-only joint.

Bluff View

As ubiquitous as the coffee-sandwich-dessert bar is these days, it is still refreshing when someone does it well. **Rembrandt's Coffee House** (204 High St., 423/265-5003, Mon.–Thurs. 7 A.M.–10 P.M., Fri. 7 A.M.–11:30 P.M., Sat. 8 A.M.–11:30 P.M., Sun. 8 A.M.–10 P.M.,

The Bluff View Art District is one of Chattanooga's best places to stroll.

$5–7) is one such place. Located catty-corner from the Hunter Museum of American Art, Rembrandt's serves excellent hot and cold sandwiches on superb locally baked bread. The menu also offers salads, including a delicious spinach salad with bacon, hard-boiled eggs, and walnuts. The ingredients are fresh and flavorful. For breakfast choose from French toast panini filled with fruit compote and mascarpone cheese, hot breakfast sandwiches, or lighter options such as bagels, yogurt and fruit, or banana bread. The coffee here is excellent, and you can finish off your meal with a wide array of sweets. Rembrandt's is not without a sense of humor. Step outside, and you will see a plate-glass window with a sign reading Working Artist. He or she will be making hand-dipped chocolate treats you can buy inside. There's a second location inside Memorial Hospital.

The setting at ◖**Back Inn Café** (412 E. 2nd St., 423/265-5033, Mon.–Fri. 7 A.M.–9 P.M., Sat. 8 A.M.–10 P.M., Sun. 8 A.M.–9 P.M., $14–28) is romantic and relaxing. Located in a stately old home, the Back Inn offers diners the choice of dining in the library, sunroom, or on the terrace overlooking the river. Polished wood floors, elegant old-world finishes, and a lovely view make you feel distinctly at home in this restaurant. The menu features global cuisine with a good wine list.

Lunchtime entrées include Japanese bento boxes, penne carbonara, and shrimp and grits. There are also salads and sandwiches, and gluten-free options. At dinner, choose from entrées such as Thai curry chicken, seafood gratin, and the house specialty Martin House steak tenderloin. Reservations are recommended.

Southside

Main Street, near the famous Choo Choo, has become one of the city's favorite dining districts. The sleek, modern **Alleia** (25 E. Main St., 423/305-6990, http://alleiarestaurant.com, Mon.–Thurs. 5–9:30 P.M., Fri.–Sat. 5–10 P.M.,

The Bluegrass Grill on artsy Main Street is a favorite for breakfast.

seafood, and meat plates. Come for an afternoon glass of wine to be enjoyed with a plate of cheese and bread. Or come for a more filling dinner; try the handcrafted spinach ravioli, fresh seafood plates, or osso buco. The restaurant's bold colors and metal sculptures give it a rustic-hip feel. In the tapas tradition, each plate is a small portion, about appetizer size, and you should order several as part of your multicourse meal. In addition to tapas, Terra Nostra has 80 different wines available by the glass and 90 available by the bottle.

For sushi, many Chattanoogans head to **Sushi Nabe** (110 River St., 423/634-0171, www.sushinabechattanooga.com, Mon. 4–9 P.M., Tues.–Thurs. and Sun. 11:30 A.M.–2:30 P.M. and 5–9:30 P.M., Fri.–Sat. 11:30 A.M.–2:30 P.M. and 5–10:30 P.M., sushi $4–7 per roll, combination plates $15–18). Located adjacent to Coolidge Park, this chic eatery offers seating at the sushi bar or at tables. In addition to sushi, you can order stir-fries and other Japanese specialties. There are also convenient dinner combination plates.

INFORMATION AND SERVICES
Visitor Information

The **Chattanooga Area Convention and Visitors Bureau** (2 Broad St., 423/756-8687 or 800/322-3344, www.chattanoogafun.com) provides information online, over the telephone, and in person at its visitors center, located right next door to the Tennessee Aquarium.

Media

The *Chattanooga Times Free Press* (www.timesfreepress.com) is the city's daily newspaper. *The Pulse* (www.chattanoogapulse.com) is a free alternative weekly paper with a focus on arts, entertainment, and culture.

Libraries

The **Chattanooga-Hamilton County Bicentennial Library** (1001 Broad St.,

$6–27) is cozy enough for date night, but not so romantic that it doesn't work for a business dinner. The wine list is impressive.

For morning meals, join the locals at **C Bluegrass Grill** (55 E. Main St., 423/752-4020, http://bluegrassgrillchattanooga.com, Tues.–Fri. 6:30 A.M.–2 P.M., Sat. 6:30 A.M.–1 P.M., $2–9). Breakfast is served whenever this homey joint is open; don't miss the homemade breads and potatoes. Look for the sign with the banjo on it.

North Shore

In recent years, the streets across the river from downtown Chattanooga have become popular locations for restaurants.

Terra Nostra Restaurant and Wine Bar (105 Frazier Ave., 423/634-0238, www.terranostratapas.com, Mon.–Thurs. 4:30–10 P.M., Fri.–Sat. 4:30–11 P.M., Sun. 4:30–9 P.M., $7–15) is a tapas restaurant with vegetarian,

© LAWRENCE MILLER

423/757-5310, Mon.–Thurs. 9 A.M.–9 P.M., Fri.–Sat. 9 A.M.–6 P.M.) is the city's main downtown library. The entire library is a wireless Internet hot spot, and there is also free Internet access on library terminals.

Laundry

Gordon's Cleaners (315 N. Market St. and 3546 Broad St., 423/265-5877) has dry cleaning and laundry service downtown.

GETTING THERE

Chattanooga is located along three major interstate highways. I-75 travels north–south from Knoxville in the north to Atlanta in the south. I-24 runs from Nashville to Chattanooga, and I-59 runs from Birmingham to Chattanooga.

Chattanooga is about 115 miles from Knoxville, 130 miles from Nashville, 120 miles from Atlanta, and 150 miles from Birmingham.

The **Chattanooga Metropolitan Airport** (CHA, 423/855-2202, www.chattairport.com) is served by a half dozen airlines providing nonstop service to nine different U.S. cities, although many people fly to either Atlanta or Nashville and take shuttles to Chattanooga.

The Chattanooga airport is located about 14 miles east of the city center. To get downtown from the airport, take Highway 153 south to I-75 and follow the signs to downtown Chattanooga.

GETTING AROUND

Chattanooga is an exceedingly pedestrian-friendly city. There is plenty of downtown parking, and it is easy to get around on foot or by the free public trolleys. You can walk from

downtown to Bluff View and even to the North Shore via the Walnut Street pedestrian bridge.

You'll need a car to get to Lookout Mountain attractions.

Public Transportation

Chattanooga's public transit service operates an electric (zero-emissions) shuttle bus service around downtown. The **CARTA Electric Shuttle** (www.carta-bus.org, runs every five minutes Mon.–Fri. 6:30 A.M.–11 P.M., Sat. 9 A.M.–11 P.M., Sun. 9 A.M.–8:30 P.M., adults $1.50, children $0.75, 24-hour unlimited-ride pass $4) runs from the Chattanooga Choo Choo building on the south side of town to the Tennessee Aquarium along the waterfront. There are stops about every block; if you need to get to a specific place, just ask your driver. Maps are posted around the city, and free guides are available at the north parking lot.

The route is convenient to all downtown hotels. There are large parking garages at both ends of the shuttle route. It costs $3 to park by the Choo Choo and $7 to park by the aquarium. Since there is no such thing as free parking anywhere around downtown Chattanooga, parking and riding the shuttle is a very good idea.

Parking

All parking around downtown Chattanooga is paid. If you find a metered space along the road, grab it, because these are the cheapest, at least for short-term parking. There are large lots located across from the Tennessee Aquarium. All-day parking will run you about $7, and evening parking will cost $5. There is a large public lot next to the Choo Choo, where all-day parking is just $3. Rates are higher during special events.

The Ocoee

The lands east of Chattanooga are speckled by towns that still bear names bestowed by some of their first settlers. Citico, Chota, Hiwassee, and Tellico were named by Overhill Cherokee who made the journey over the mountains and into southeastern Tennessee during the 17th century. Red Clay State Historic Park was the site of the last council meeting of the Cherokee before their forced removal in 1838. Today, these lands are part of the southern portion of the Cherokee National Forest, an expanse of 300,000 acres of federal lands that contain rivers, mountains, and rural farmland.

The southern part of the Cherokee National Forest is defined by the powerful Ocoee River, which attracts thrill-seeking rafters and kayakers. Sightseers enjoy scenic drives up Chilhowee Mountain and along the river, past recreation areas and opportunities for hiking and swimming.

Several towns in the southeastern corner of this region have strong mining histories. Ducktown, Copperhill, and Coker Creek are among the quiet towns that now preserve their unique history with museums and historic tours.

The Hiwassee River cuts through the national forest north of the Ocoee, passing the historic town of Reliance and posing opportunities for laid-back canoe and raft outings.

CLEVELAND

Cleveland is one gateway to the Cherokee National Forest. The seat of Bradley County, Cleveland is home to Lee University, a four-year Christian college operated by the Church of God, as well as the Church of God Theological Seminary, a graduate school for Christian ministry.

Sights

Find your way to Johnston Park downtown to see the **Cherokee Chieftain,** a large sculpture carved by Peter "Wolf" Toth. The sculpture was presented to the city of Cleveland in 1974 and represents the close association this region has with the Cherokee people.

The **Museum Center at Five Points** (200 Inman St., 423/339-5745, www.museumcenter.org, Tues.–Fri. 10 A.M.–5 P.M., Sat. 10 A.M.–3 P.M., adults $5, children $4) is a history museum dedicated to telling the story of the different groups of people who have lived along the Ocoee River. The museum is located at the end of the Old Copper Trail, the road by which copper traveled from the Copper Basin, through the mountains, and to the railroad at Cleveland.

Accommodations

The **Whitewater Lodge** (2500 Pointe South Rd., 423/479-7811, $30) is a bit far from the action of the Ocoee River, but the price can't be beat. Rooms have a kitchenette with coffeemaker, sink, and stovetop, adding to the bargain. Weekly rates are also available.

COLLEGEDALE

More than 200 ancient artifacts from the Near East are on exhibit at the **Lynn H. Wood Archaeological Museum** (Industrial Dr., Southern Adventist University, 423/236-2030, http://archaeology.southern.edu, Tues.–Thurs. 9 A.M.–noon and 1–5 P.M., Fri. 9–11 A.M., Sat.–Sun. 2–5 P.M., free). Museum curators strive to depict life in the Biblical world with artifacts from Egypt, Babylonia, Persia, Syria-Palestine, Greece, Cyprus, and Anatolia. Highlights include a complete series of lamps from the Chalcolithic to early Arabic periods and handwritten cuneiform tablets from Ur.

RED CLAY STATE HISTORIC PARK

Red Clay State Historic Park (1140 Red Clay Park Rd., 423/478-0339, daily 8 A.M.–sunset,

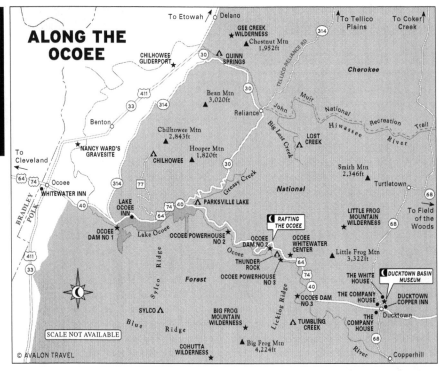

ALONG THE OCOEE

$3 per vehicle) was the site of the Cherokee capital from 1832 to 1838. In the years leading up to 1832, the State of Georgia outlawed Cherokee councils, so in 1832 the Cherokee moved their capital from New Echota, Georgia, to Red Clay, Tennessee, just over the state line. As many as 5,000 people attended the 11 council meetings held here until 1838, the year of the Cherokee's forced removal via the Trail of Tears. It was here at Red Clay that many Cherokee first learned of the planned removal.

The park consists of a **visitors center** (Mon.–Sat. 8 A.M.–4:30 P.M., Sun. 1–4:30 P.M.), re-created Cherokee settlement and council house, and a permanent exhibit on the Cherokee culture. The most prominent natural landmark is the spring, which rises from beneath a limestone ledge to form a deep pool that flows into Mill Creek, a tributary of the Conasauga and Coosa River system. The spring is about 15 feet deep and produces more than 500,000 gallons of water each day.

The park is an official interpretive center on the National Historic Trail of Tears. Cherokee Days of Recognition is held on the first weekend of August each year. It includes authentic Cherokee crafts, food, storytelling, and music.

OCOEE

The town of Ocoee is a smattering of businesses and homes located on Highways 64 and 411.

A few miles north of the intersection, along Highway 411, is the **Gravesite of Nancy Ward,** located atop a small hill. There is a parking area and pathway to the summit. Nancy Ward was born in 1738 at the Cherokee town of Chota, and she was named Nanye-hi. Nanye-hi had a queenly appearance and commanding bearing,

THE CHEROKEE NATIONAL FOREST

The Cherokee National Forest covers 640,000 acres of land on the eastern edge of Tennessee. The southern portion extends from the Georgia state line all the way to the southern boundary of the Great Smoky Mountains National Park, encompassing some 300,000 acres. The northern portion—which covers 327,000 acres—ranges from the northern boundary of the Smokies to the Virginia state line.

The federal government began buying land in East Tennessee around 1912. The government's action was in response to the environmental effects of widespread logging in the southern mountains. Clear-cutting, erosion, and wildfires ravaged the environment, and the federal government stepped in to preserve the headwaters of area rivers. In 1920, President Woodrow Wilson declared the lands to be the Cherokee National Forest, and in 1936 the boundaries were redrawn to put the forest entirely within the state of Tennessee (Pisgah and Natahala National Forests were established in North Carolina). During the New Deal, the Civilian Conservation Corps (CCC) built many of the trails that still exist today in the forest, and the Tennessee Valley Authority built dams and reservoirs.

National forests differ from national parks in several important ways. The motto of the forest service is "Caring for the land and serving the people," a statement that reveals its dual purpose. So while environmental stewardship is one objective of park managers, they are also concerned with encouraging recreation and the use of natural resources. Activities such as off-road mountain biking, hunting, and logging—which are not permitted in the Great Smoky Mountains National Park—are allowed in the Cherokee National Forest. Equally significant, commercial and residential development is allowed in certain parts of the national forest.

Some 66,000 acres of the forest is classified as wilderness, a designation that prohibits logging, motorized vehicles, construction, and development. Some 20,000 acres are classified as scenic, a designation that prohibits logging and allows only limited vehicle use. Meanwhile, 46,000 acres have been classified as primitive, which opens them up to low-impact recreation in a nonmotorized environment. There is a recurring tension between those who want more environmental protection in the forest and those who want to open the lands up to more intensive uses and development.

Despite this, the Cherokee National Forest remains a beautiful, ecologically rich, and—in some parts—wild area. The forest is home to some 120 bird species, including wild turkey, golden eagle, and peregrine falcon; 47 mammal species, including the black bear, red wolf, wild boar, and coyote; and 30 species of reptile, including rattlesnake, copperhead, and salamander. It is home to many endangered species, including the northern flying squirrel and two varieties of river mussels.

Hiking, camping, horseback riding, swimming, boating, white-water sports, and biking are just a few of the activities that draw people to the Cherokee National Forest.

The supervisor's office for the entire forest—north and south—is at 2800 North Ocoee Street in Cleveland. Call them at 423/476-9700. The southern forest has two ranger districts and corresponding ranger stations. The **Ocoee/Hiwassee District** (3171 Hwy. 64, 423/338-5201) is located along the Ocoee River near Benton. The **Tellico Ranger Station** (250 Ranger Station Rd., 423/253-2520) is located along the Cherohala Skyway near Tellico Plains.

The northern forest has two ranger stations. The **Nolichucky/Unaka District Ranger Station** (4900 Asheville Hwy./State Rte. 70, 423/638-4109) is located near Greeneville. The **Watauga District Ranger Station** (4400 Unicoi Dr., Unicoi, 423/735-1500) is in Unicoi. Ranger stations are generally open daily 8:30 A.M.-4:30 P.M., and they are the best places to buy maps and get other information about recreation in the national forest. You can also visit the online store maintained by the Cradle of Forestry (www.cradleofforestry.com).

and she fought alongside her husband and other men in a raid on the Creeks during the 1755 Battle of Taliwa. Ward was chosen as *Agi-gau-u-e* (Beloved Woman) of the Cherokee. As such, she sat on the Council of Chiefs, had complete power over prisoners, and led the Women's Council.

In the late 1750s, an English trader named Bryant Ward moved in to the area and married Nancy, as she was called by the white settlers, although he already had a wife and family in South Carolina. They had a daughter, Betsy, who joined Five Killer and Catherine, children of Ward's first marriage, as her offspring.

Ward was influential in her tribe and with the white settlers. She advocated peace between Indians and settlers, and more than once she warned settlers of an impending Indian attack. She spoke at the negotiations held on the Long Island of the Holston and at the Treaty of Hopewell.

With the Hiwassee Purchase of 1819, Ward along with all Cherokee was forced to abandon Chota, their capital city of Overhill Tennessee. She moved south and settled near where her gravesite lies today. Ward died in 1822.

The oldest monument at Ward's gravesite was erected in 1923 by the Nancy Ward Chapter of the Daughters of the American Revolution. Newer exhibits by the Tennessee Overhill Association detail her life.

Accommodations

The **Whitewater Inn** (120 Whitewater Dr., 423/338-1201, www.ocoeewhitewaterinn.com, $63–103) is a standard-issue motel that still has a good deal of polish left. Designed to feel a bit like a mountain lodge, this inn offers comfortable rooms with two queen-size beds, satellite TV, and telephones. There is free continental breakfast, wireless Internet, and fax and copy service. Rates are higher in season. Apartments with a full kitchen ($150) are also available.

ALONG THE OCOEE

Just past Ocoee on Highway 64, you enter the Cherokee National Forest. The next 26 miles are a winding two-lane blacktop that follows the Ocoee River.

Chilhowee Mountain

For breathtaking views of Parksville Lake, the Ocoee River, and the Great Eastern Valley of Tennessee, take a seven-mile detour up Forest Service Road 77 to the summit of Chilhowee Mountain. There are no fewer than five overlooks on the drive, which terminates at the Cumberland Recreation Area, a day-use facility and campground. There is also a historical marker that recalls the Confederate soldiers who camped in these hills and waged guerilla war on Unionists during the Civil War.

Once at the Cumberland Recreation Area, you can hike 1.5 miles to **Benton Falls** or take any of the seven other trails in the area. There is also a swimming beach, bathhouses, and picnic tables.

Parksville Lake

This nearly 2,000-acre lake formed by the Ocoee River is operated as a Forest Service recreation area. There is a swimming beach, campground, picnic area, and boat launches. The lake is popular for fishing, waterskiing, and riding personal watercraft.

Ocoee River Dams

The Tennessee Valley Authority operates three powerhouses along the Ocoee River, which together produce some 70,000 kilowatts of electricity. Ocoee 1, the westernmost facility, predates TVA and forms the Parksville Lake (also called the Ocoee Lake). There is a marker and overlook next to the dam, which was built in 1910.

Ocoee 2 was built in 1913 and consists of a diversion dam, wooden flume, and powerhouse. When the powerhouse is on, the river water is diverted into the flume, which carries it five miles downstream to the Ocoee 2

HIKING IN THE SOUTHERN CHEROKEE

If you plan to do much hiking in the southern Cherokee National Forest, you should invest in good boots, a water bottle, a GPS, and a good trail map. The best is National Geographic's Trails Illustrated No. 781 *Tellico and Ocoee River Cherokee National Forest.*

There are dozens of hiking trails in the southern Cherokee National Forest. The following are some of the best.

The **Old Copper Trail** begins at the Ocoee Whitewater Center and is a 2.3-mile (one-way) hike along an old mining road. The Old Copper Trail is the last remaining portion of a road that was built around 1851 to connect the copper-mining towns of Ducktown and Copperhill with Cleveland. It took miners two days to haul the copper by mule the 33 miles to Cleveland. When Highway 64 was built in the 1930s, it followed the old Copper Road route, and subsequent upgrades widened and improved the current highway.

The present-day hiking trail follows the edge of the river, passing apple trees and stone foundations left by farm families, some of whom were Cherokee Indians, in the early 19th century. You'll also pass a beaver pond and cross four footbridges, including three timber stringer plank bridges and one heavy timber bridge.

Other hikes that start at the Whitewater Center include **Bear Paw Loop** (1.7 miles) and the **Chestnut Mountain Loop** (6 miles).

One of the most famous trails in the forest is the **Benton MacKaye Trail** (www.bmta. org), a 150-mile trail named for the creator of the Appalachian Trail (AT). When the AT was getting congested, a group of dedicated hikers set out to create a new long-haul hike through the Southern mountains. The Benton MacKaye Trail begins at Spring Mountain, Georgia, as does the AT. It follows a different path, however, and ends at Davenport Gap, North Carolina, in the Great Smoky Mountains National Park. The trail enters the Cherokee National Forest at Big Frog Mountain. Access points are at Forest Service Road 221, Forest Service Road 45, Thunder Rock Campground, and Highway 64 across from Ocoee Powerhouse No. 3.

Benton Falls Trail is an easy 1.5-mile (one-way) trail that leaves from Chilhowee Campground and follows Rock Creek to 65-foot Benton Falls.

The **John Muir Trail** covers 18.8 miles along the Hiwassee River from Childers Creek near Reliance to Highway 68 at Farmer. The trail follows a route described by naturalist and writer John Muir in his book *A Thousand Mile Walk to the Gulf.*

The **Oswald Dome Trail** climbs 3.9 miles up Bean Mountain from the Quinn Springs Campground on Highway 30 near Reliance. The trail ends at an elevation of 3,500 feet near the Oswald Dome fire tower.

Lastly, the **Unicoi Turnpike Trail** is a 2.5-mile portion of the historic Unicoi Turnpike, an old road that settlers, hunters, and Native Americans used to get over the mountains. The trail connects Doc Rogers Fields near Coker Creek with the Unicoi Gap. Along the way you will see a marker for a murdered tollgate keeper and the remnants of Rolling Stone Civilian Conservation Corps (CCC) Camp.

---

powerhouse, where it is dropped from a height of 250 feet, creating far more power than it would otherwise. The flume, which is visible as you drive along the river, is on the National Register of Historic Places. Ocoee 3, built in 1942, follows a similar pattern. It has a diversion dam, a tunnel, and a powerhouse.

When the river water is being used to generate electricity, the Ocoee River is just a trickle down a dry riverbed. But TVA releases water for recreation on certain days of the year, according to a published schedule. A one-mile section below Ocoee 3 is the Olympic whitewater section, and it passes in front of the Ocoee Whitewater Center. A four-mile segment below Ocoee 2 is used by commercial outfitters and water-sports enthusiasts for rafting and kayaking trips.

The Ocoee River was not always recognized as a site for white-water sports. In fact, it was

BIKING IN THE SOUTHERN CHEROKEE

Mountain biking is permitted on dozens of trails within the Cherokee National Forest, making this a popular destination for off-road bicyclists. The **Chilhowee Mountain Bike Trail System** is centered in the Chilhowee Mountain recreation area, near the town of Ocoee. It includes nine different trails ranging from easy to advanced. The two-mile Azalea Trail is a favorite; the 5.4-mile Clear Creek Trail is challenging, with wrenching uphill and screaming downhill segments.

The **Tanasi Mountain Bike Trail System** is located near the Ocoee Whitewater Center and has five trails, including the 11.5-mile advanced Chestnut Mountain-West Fork Loop. The Thunder Rock Express is a 1.5-mile stretch of trail with exciting downhill segments and lots of jumps. The Tanasi system is so revered by mountain bikers that a top-of-the-line titanium-frame mountain bike is named after it.

Elite road bikers head to the **Cherohala Skyway** for endurance rides. The road climbs for 21 miles on the Tennessee side before beginning a 15-mile descent in North Carolina. Steep switchbacks and high elevation make this a challenging ride for even the most experienced bikers. The Skyway is the location of the 100-mile **Cherohala Challenge** every June.

The **Tellico Ranger District Trail System,** north of the Cherohala Skyway, includes the 11-mile Citico Creek and Tellico River Trail, a challenging ride along a gravel road, and the Indian Boundary Loop, a 3.2-mile level track that circles Indian Boundary Lake.

Bike rentals and gear are available from **Trailhead Bicycle Company** (225 1st St. NE, Cleveland, 423/472-9899), which offers superior gear and repair services.

Copperhill's **Ocoee Adventure Center** (4654 Hwy. 64, 423/496-4437, www.ocoeeadventurecenter.com) offers guided mountain bike trips and personalized instruction. Rates are $45 per person for a half-day, and $89 per person for a whole day. **Outdoor Adventure Rafting** (629 Welcome Valley Rd., 423/338-5746, www.raft.com) near Benton rents bikes for $15 per hour or $40 per day and will also create custom bike trips for your group.

---

only due to the deterioration of the Ocoee 2 water flume that the river's recreational potential was discovered. It was around 1976 that years of weathering caused TVA to shut down the flume for repairs, causing river water to flow unimpeded down the Ocoee for the first time in decades.

It did not take long for the first daredevils to discover the thrill of the rapids; the first river riders rode Navy surplus rafts. The first two outfitters, Ocoee Outdoors and Sunburst Expeditions, opened their doors in 1977.

But meanwhile TVA was repairing the flume, and in 1984 it was ready to again divert the river water away from the riverbed. By this time, however, the rafting industry had blossomed. So in 1984 the Outfitters Association and TVA reached a 35-year agreement where rafting companies would get a minimum of 116 days of rafting water each year and would pay $2 per customer to compensate TVA for the loss of power generation. It is an agreement that has allowed TVA to continue operation and the rafting industry to flourish.

◖ Rafting the Ocoee

White-water rafting is the most popular activity of the southern Cherokee Forest between June and September. The four miles between the Ocoee 2 diversion dam and the Ocoee 2 powerhouse are where the fun happens, over 20 different rapids with names like Grumpy, Broken Nose, Double Suck, Slingshot, and Hell's Hole.

The Ocoee River is for experienced or adventurous outdoorspeople. With Class III–IV rapids, the river can be frightening or dangerous if you're not experienced or confident enough. No one under 12 is permitted to raft anywhere

COURTESY OF CHATTANOOGA VISITOR'S BUREAU

There are few better ways to catch a buzz than rafting the Ocoee River.

Don't carry anything with you, like a camera, that can't be submerged. In summer, wear your bathing suit, shorts, a T-shirt, and tennis shoes. During the cooler months, suit up in a wet suit or wear a windbreaker or wool sweater to keep warm. Wool socks and tennis shoes are also nice. Regardless of the season, avoid cotton clothing and bring a change of clothes to put on after your trip. Most rafting companies offer somewhere to store your belongings until after the trip.

There are more than 20 companies offering rafting trips down the Ocoee. Some of the best are **Ocoee Rafting** (Ducktown, 423/496-3388, www.ocoeerafting.com), **Nantahala Outdoor Center (NOC)** (13077 U.S. 19, Bryson City NC, 423/338-5901, www.noc.com), and **Ocoee Inn Rafting** (2496 Hwy. 64, 423/338-2064, www.ocoeeinn.com).

If you want to make a more significant commitment to the sport of kayaking, sign up for a clinic at **Ocoee Adventure Center** (4651 Hwy. 64, 423/496-4437, www.ocoeeadventurecenter.com) or NOC.

on the Ocoee. Beginners or families with young children should raft down the Hiwassee instead. If you are uncertain, talk to an experienced outfitter about which rafting trip would be best for your group.

Watching as other people make their way down the river is also an enjoyable pastime. Places where you can pull over and parking areas along the rafting portion of the river are often full of onlookers on summer afternoons and other busy periods.

The Ocoee rafting and floating season runs March–September. During the spring and fall, outfitters will offer trips on weekends or holidays only. During the summer, there are trips every day. Rafting on the river is dependent on TVA's schedule of water releases. You can pick up a schedule from the Ocoee Whitewater Center (Hwy. 64 W., 423/496-5197, www.fs.fed.us/r8/ocoee).

When you go rafting, do plan to get wet.

OCOEE WHITEWATER CENTER

Built for the 1996 Atlanta Summer Olympics, the Ocoee Whitewater Center (Hwy. 64 W., 423/496-5197, www.fs.fed.us/r8/ocoee, Apr.–Nov. daily 9 A.M.–5 P.M., Thanksgiving–Mar. Fri.–Sun. 9 A.M.–5 P.M., free) is a central source of information about the Ocoee River, has restrooms and other amenities, and is a starting point for several hikes.

The riverbed in front of the center is pockmarked and rugged; the natural contours of the river were "improved" in preparation for the Olympics. When the water is low, children and adults will enjoy walking around the pools and streams on the riverbed or sunning on the rocks. When the water is high, marvel at the power and sound of fast-running water while you watch rafters and kayakers maneuvering down the rapids.

There are rocking chairs and plenty of benches around for relaxing. The Olympic

Legacy Bridge spans the river, providing nice views of the water below. During spring and summer, plan to walk through the gardens, which showcase native plants. You can find a guide to the gardens at the visitors center, which has great additional information about the area.

Visitors to the center can park for 30 minutes in the lot right next to the center. Long-term users must park below and pay a fee of $3 per vehicle.

Accommodations

The **C** **Lake Ocoee Inn** (2496 Hwy. 64, 423/338-2064, www.ocoeeinn.com, $55–65) is located about 15 miles west of the Ocoee Whitewater Center and sits on the shore of placid Lake Ocoee (Parksville Lake). This motel opened in 1936 and has nondescript motel rooms, plus four fully equipped cabins. There is also a marina. Generally speaking, Lake Ocoee attracts an outdoorsy crowd. It is also family friendly.

Practicalities

Gas, food, and lodging are somewhat limited along the Ocoee River. There are **gas stations** at Ocoee, Ducktown, and at Greasy Creek, about five miles up Highway 30. There are restaurants in Ocoee, Ducktown, and Copper Hill, plus one restaurant along the river. The best way to handle food during a trip to the river is to pack a picnic lunch and enjoy it at one of the many picnic areas in the forest. There are modest groceries in Greasy Creek, Reliance, and Ocoee. In Ducktown, there's a **Piggly Wiggly** (125 Five Points Dr.).

DUCKTOWN

Ducktown, and its sister city Copperhill, are the heart of the Copper Basin of Tennessee. Here, copper was mined from the 1850s until the 1980s.

In order to fuel the copper smelters, timber was harvested all around. By 1876, all the trees in the area were gone, and logs had to be floated in from Fannin County, Georgia. Between 1865 and 1878, 24 million pounds of copper were removed from the earth and 50 square miles of the basin had been stripped of its trees.

The area's mines declined between 1878 and 1890, until a new railroad spur arrived in the area. In 1899 the Tennessee Copper Company opened the Burra Burra Mine in Ducktown and built a new smelter. During this period, mining companies used an open roasting process to remove copper from the raw ore. This open roasting required lots of timber for fuel, and it let off sulfuric acid, which killed vegetation and left the landscape eerily empty. Acid rain fell, polluting the Ocoee River and other nearby bodies of water.

The environmental abuse of more than a century left its mark on Tennessee's Copper Basin. For years, this area was distinctive for its barren orange-red hills and craters, the legacy of many years of deforestation and the open release of sulfuric acid. Residents had mixed feelings about the landscape—it was strangely beautiful, but at the same time it was a constant reminder of environmental damage. There were also concerns about health effects. Early efforts to reforest the old mines date back to the early 20th century, but it was not until the 1970s that scientists figured out a way to successfully introduce trees back into the denuded landscape. Since then, pine trees have grown to cover virtually all of the hills that were once barren.

Copper was mined here until 1987, and the plant at Copperhill still processes sulfur, although the raw materials are trucked in—not mined.

Ducktown was a company town, a fact that is evident as you take a short drive around. Main Street is little more than two blocks with a handful of elegant homes built by mine owners and bosses. The main residential neighborhood is a collection of modest homes in a slight hollow. The newer parts of town, including gas stations, motels, and a school, are found near the intersection of Highways 64 and 68.

CAMPING IN THE SOUTHERN CHEROKEE

There are more than a dozen developed campgrounds in the southern region of the Cherokee National Forest. Campgrounds vary from developed areas with electrical hookups for RVs and hot showers to rustic grounds with chemical toilets and no shower facilities at all. Most Forest Service campgrounds are open mid-March–December, although some are available year-round, and most are open on a first-come, first-served basis. Where reservations are available, they must be made through the government's centralized reservation service at www.reserveusa.com or by calling 877/444-6777.

Camping rates range $10-20 depending on the type of site you choose and the popularity of the campground. The following are some of the most popular campgrounds; for a complete list, contact the nearest ranger station.

OCOEE/HIWASSEE DISTRICT

The largest campground is **Chilhowee Recreation Area,** located along Forest Service Road 77. There are 86 campsites, warm showers, and flush toilets. You are next door to the McKamy Lake beach and have easy access to 25 miles of hike/bike trails.

Thunder Rock is located near Ocoee Powerhouse No. 3 and is convenient to the Whitewater Center. There are 39 sites, warm showers, and flush toilets. This is a popular campsite for rafters and other water-sports enthusiasts.

Parksville Lake, open April 1-October 31, is located along Rock Creek and has 17 campsites, warm showers, and flush toilets. It is convenient to the white-water section of the Ocoee River and to swimming, boating, and fishing on Parksville Lake.

Lost Creek, located off Highway 30 near Reliance, has 15 sites and is set in a mature hardwood forest next to Big Lost Creek. It is a peaceful and wild area, but the flush toilets and hot showers provide basic creature comforts. RVs are welcome.

TELLICO DISTRICT

Big Oak Cove is an 11-site campground located on the banks of the Tellico River. A retreat for tent campers, the grounds are open mid-March–December. Hiking, fishing, and wading are available nearby. The fee is $10 per night. There are chemical toilets and cold showers.

Located off the Cherohala Skyway at an elevation of 1,800 feet, **Holly Flats** is an 18-site tent-friendly campsite with limited facilities. There are chemical toilets and cold showers, but little in the way of other comforts. The setting is peaceful and typically uncrowded.

One of the most popular campgrounds in this part of the forest is **Indian Boundary,** an 88-site campground located on Indian Boundary Lake along the Cherohala Skyway. Four loops offer various levels of comfort, from full RV hookups to rustic tent sites. Recreation includes hiking or biking around the lake, boating, fishing, and swimming. Reservations are accepted.

◖ Ducktown Basin Museum

The Ducktown Basin Museum (212 Burra Burra St., 423/496-5778, Mon.–Sat. 10 A.M.–4:30 P.M., hours may be extended 30 minutes in summer, adults $4, seniors $3, children $0.50) captures the unique history and culture of Tennessee's Copper Basin. Located in the offices of the old Burra Burra Mine, the museum has displays about the historical development of the mines, the culture that developed in the company towns, and the mining business itself. Special topics include mine safety, the railroad, and the history of strikes at the mine. The visit includes a 15-minute video that tells the story of the entire region and describes the three periods during which the hills here were mined for copper and other minerals.

At the rear of the museum is one of the only "copper craters" that was not reforested. Although volunteer pine trees are beginning to take root in the red soil, you can still imagine how distinctive the landscape once looked.

Accommodations

Ducktown is close enough to the Ocoee and several outdoor outfitters to make it a popular

© DUCKTOWN BASIN MUSEUM

Learn about the history of copper mining at the Ducktown Basin Museum.

place for outdoor thrill seekers. But the additional draw of the mining museum is another reason to make this your home base in the Overhill region.

For a bed-and-breakfast option in Ducktown, try **The Company House** (125 Main St., 423/496-5634, www.bbonline.com/tn/companyhouse, $89–99). It has six guest rooms, each named for a mine in the area. All rooms have private baths and in-room telephones.

If motel lodging is more your thing, then there are two options. The **Ducktown Copper Inn** (U.S. 64 and Hwy. 68, 423/496-5541, $55–65) is an aging motel with no-frills accommodations. Rooms have microwaves, refrigerators, and televisions. The **Ocoee River Inn** (5082 Hwy. 64, 877/546-2633, $60–80) is a newer outfit, with many of the same amenities (but less grunge) than its nearby neighbor.

Food

With the exception of a gas-station convenience store, **Brother's Copper Kettle** (5750 Hwy. 64, 423/496-5001, Mon.–Sat. 11 A.M.–9 P.M., $4–12) is the only game in town. The menu includes a buffet, salad bar, and barbecue sandwiches.

COPPERHILL

Copperhill sits on the state line and on the banks of the Ocoee River. On the Georgia side, the town is called McCaysville and the river is called the Toccoa.

There is more going on in Copperhill than Ducktown, due largely to the scenic train excursions that stop here for midday layovers. A pleasant main street district with restaurants and shops makes this a nice place to spend an hour or so. Walk up the hillside that faces Ocoee Street for views of the town and the Ocoee/Toccoa River.

Rail Excursions

In addition to the rail excursions offered by the Tennessee Valley Railroad, the **Blue Ridge**

Scenic Railway (241 Depot St., Blue Ridge, GA, 706/632-9833, www.brscenic.com, adults $28–43, children about half price) offers railroad excursions that come to Copperhill. The trip leaves from Blue Ridge, Georgia, and makes a one-hour journey north through the mountains to Copperhill, where you have two hours to eat and shop.

Food

More than 70 years after its founding, the **New York Restaurant** (121 Ocoee St., 423/496-3855, www.thenewyorkrestaurant.com, daily 7 A.M.–3 P.M., $2–6) was remodeled and came under new management in 2007. You can eat at the classic lunch counter or dine on white tablecloths at a table.

The menu includes plate lunches of hamburger steak, chicken breast and gravy, or chicken salad, and sandwiches including tuna melts and Philly cheesesteaks. There are some modern additions, too: hummus in pita and black-bean veggie burgers. If you prefer omelets and eggs, order from the breakfast menu all day. After a day rafting the river, you'll appreciate that beer is served.

TURTLETOWN

Drive north from Ducktown on Highway 68 to find more quiet towns and rural countryside.

Just beyond the small community of Turtletown, Highway 294 splits off Highway 68, headed toward North Carolina. About four miles down this road, and about two miles past the state line, there is a remarkable monument to the Christian faith. **Fields of the Wood Bible Park** (10000 Hwy. 294, Murphy NC, 828/494-7855, www.fieldsofthewoodbiblepark.com, daily sunrise–sunset, free) is a project of the Church of God of Prophecy that contains, among other things, the world's largest cross and the largest representation of the Ten Commandments. The latter is located just inside the park's gates and is laid out on a hillside. Each letter spelling out the commandments is five feet high and four feet wide. This is just the beginning of what Fields of the Wood has to offer. You will also find replicas of Joseph's tomb, where Christ was buried and rose from the dead, and Golgotha, where Jesus offered himself as a sacrifice. There is also a gift shop and the Burger Mountain Café, which are open Monday–Saturday 9 A.M.–5 P.M.

The Hiwassee

Named from the Cherokee word *ayuwasi* (savannah or meadow), the Hiwassee River drains fertile agricultural lands and passes through the heartland of the southern Cherokee National Forest.

RELIANCE

The Reliance historic district is located along the Hiwassee River, near where Highways 30 and 315 intersect. The **Hiwassee Union Church** is a two-story board structure built jointly by the local Masonic lodge and the Union Church in 1899. On the north side of the river is the **Higdon Hotel,** also built around 1899.

Your pit stop in Reliance should be the **Webb Brothers Texaco** (3708 Hwy. 30, 423/338-2373, www.webbbros.com), a gas station, post office, general store, river outfitter, and community hub. Inside the shop you'll find a placard with historical information about Reliance.

Reliance is located about 10 miles north of the Ocoee River, along Highway 30. The drive south follows Greasy Creek, a pretty, clear stream that defies its name. You will pass old wood-frame houses and farms that have been in this valley for generations.

HIWASSEE SCENIC RIVER STATE PARK

A 23-mile section of the Hiwassee River has been designated a Tennessee Scenic River.

From Highway 411 to the North Carolina state line, the Hiwassee River offers prime opportunities for canoeing, rafting, fishing, hiking, and wildlife viewing.

Hiwassee Scenic River State Park (404 Spring Creek Rd., Delano, 423/263-0050, www.tn.gov/environment/parks/Hiwassee) and the neighboring **Gee Creek Campground** (Spring Creek Rd., Delano, 423/263-0050) are good places to come to explore the river. There are picnic grounds, restrooms, and boat-launch areas. The Gee Creek Campground has 47 particularly tent-friendly campsites, some of which are right next to the river. As is the case with Tennessee state parks, campsites are available on a first-come, first-served basis only.

Fishing is popular along the river; anglers frequently catch rainbow and brown trout, largemouth bass, yellow perch, and catfish.

Unlike the Ocoee River, the Hiwassee is a calm river, with Class I–II (rather than III–IV) rapids. Children six and up are allowed on the Hiwassee.

Because the Hiwassee is calmer, many people rent the necessary equipment and make the journey downriver without a guide. Expect to pay $40 and up per day for a six-person raft or $24 per day for a one-person Duckie. Inner tubes and other equipment are also available. Hiwassee outfitters include **Hiwassee Scenic Outfitters, Inc.** (155 Ellis Creek Rd., Reliance, 423/338-8115, www.hiwasseeoutfitters.com) and **Webb Brothers Float Service** (Reliance, 423/338-2373, www.webbbros.com).

SANDHILL CRANES

Located along the Hiwassee River between Dayton and Birchwood, the **Blythe Ferry Unit of the Hiwassee Refuge** (423/614-3018) is a good place for bird-watching. Besides seasonal shorebirds, waders, and common waterfowl such as wintering ducks and geese, the unit has become a winter stopover for migrating sandhill and whooping cranes. The concentration has grown from just a few birds to more than 6,000 at times, making this one of Tennessee's premier wildlife spectacles November–March. The refuge is closed to the public during the winter except for a Sandhill Crane Festival in January, but viewing is possible along the roads and from an observation deck.

To get to the refuge, find the junction between Highways 58 and 60 near Georgetown. Drive 7.8 miles west on Highway 60 and turn right at the wildlife sign.

The best way to get up close to the cranes and other wildlife of the Hiwassee Refuge is aboard **Blue Moon Cruises** (5637 Hwy. 411, Benton, 888/993-2583, www.bluemooncruises.org, Dec.–Mar., $40), which depart from Sale Creek Marina near Soddy-Daisy. For 3.5 hours you will ply the waters of the Hiwassee on a naturalist-led tour that includes viewing of sandhill cranes.

DELANO

Located on the edge of the national forest, between Etowah and Benton, the town of Delano is known for **Delano Daylilies** (153 County Rd. 854, 423/263-9323, www.delanodaylilies.com, late May–early June Tues.–Sat. 10 A.M.–5 P.M., free), a noteworthy seasonal attraction and nursery. This nursery raises some 1,300 varieties of colorful daylilies, and from late May to early June every year their garden is busy with area growers shopping for blooms. Casual visitors are also welcome to come and enjoy a stroll throughout the patches of daylilies, but you'll be hard-pressed not to wind up with at least one plant in your possession by the end of your visit. A covered pavilion is a lovely place to sit and relax while your traveling companion chooses lilies. There are also benches throughout the gardens.

An 1861 barn provides the centerpiece for the 11,000 acres of vineyard at **Savannah Oaks Winery** (1817 Delano Rd., 423/263-2762, www.savannah-oaks-winery.com,

Mon.–Thurs. 10 A.M.–6 P.M., Fri.–Sat. 10 A.M.–7 P.M., Sun. 1–6 P.M., free). Tours and wine and cheese tastings are available by appointment, and in the summer the winery hosts a number of events with live music.

Gliding

Gliding is flying without an engine, and you can experience this sublime form of travel at **Chilhowee Glideport** (Hwy. 411, 423/388-2000, www.chilhowee.com), near Benton. A half-hour ride costs $219 and takes you high above the scenic Cherokee National Forest and the Hiwassee and Ocoee Rivers. Chilhowee Glideport also offers lessons and rentals for gliding enthusiasts.

COKER CREEK

Before copper was mined in the Copper Basin, this area was famous for its gold. The Cherokee Indians had known about the gold for years, but whites discovered it around 1825. It didn't take long for a full-fledged gold rush to begin. Trouble was that the gold was on Cherokee land. When the Indians complained to the federal government in 1826, the U.S. army established a garrison here supposedly to enforce the Cherokee's land rights. Even the presence of soldiers did little to keep settlers from tapping into the Cherokee's resources, and the pressure from people such as these was probably one thing that sealed the Cherokee's later fate.

Sights

For the best views of this part of the Cherokee Forest, drive to **Buck Bald,** the site of an old fire tower. The tower was removed in the 1970s, but the site remains a place to enjoy 360-degree views of the surrounding landscape. To get there, drive seven miles south of Coker Creek along Highway 68, then turn left onto Buck Bald Road. It is 2.5 miles to the top.

A designated scenic area with four waterfalls and several miles of hiking trails, **Coker Creek**

Scenic Area and Falls is a wonderful place for a picnic. The four waterfalls—Upper Coker Creek Falls, Coker Creek Falls, Hiding Place Falls, and Lower Coker Creek Falls—are all located within a quarter mile of the parking area. There are picnic tables, but no toilets or potable water.

To find the falls, drive south of Coker Creek 3.1 miles along Highway 68. Turn right onto County Road 628 (Ironsburg Road) and travel 0.8 mile. Veer left at the Ironsburg Cemetery onto County Road 626 (Duckett Ridge Road) and travel for three miles. The road will become gravel. Turn left onto Forest Service Road 2138 and travel one mile to the parking area.

Festivals and Events

Since 1968 Coker Creek's **Autumn Gold Festival** (www.cokercreek.org) has been the community's largest event of the year. Taking place during the second full weekend of October—while the autumn leaves are on full display—the festival includes a crafts fair, gold panning, and the crowning of the Autumn Gold Queen.

Shopping

Coker Creek is home to several art galleries. **Designs by Baerreis** (12203 Hwy. 68, 423/261-2731, www.climbingbear.com) is a family-owned gallery showcasing the work of Phil and Martha Baerreis as well as their children. Highlights include Phil's hand-turned wooden boxes and custom-made jewelry by Elisabeth Baerreis. The **Coker Creek Gallery** (206 Hot Water Rd., 423/261-2157), located just a few hundred yards from Highway 68, has wind chimes, pottery, glass and metal sculptures, jewelry, and more.

Panning for Gold

Although the gold industry petered out at Coker Creek after the Civil War, hobby mining and panning continues. You can buy panning supplies at the **Coker Creek Welcome Center** (Hwy. 68, 423/261-2286, www.cokercreek.org).

It's unlikely that anyone will tell you the best places to pan for gold, but the most popular are easy to find. You can pan at **Coker Creek** just 0.3 mile from the welcome center, near Doc Rogers Field. **Coker Creek Falls**, eight miles south of the welcome center, is also a nice place to pan, although you may soon grow weary of the work and choose to enjoy the falls and swimming hole instead.

ETOWAH

Etowah didn't much exist until 1902, when the Louisville and Nashville Railroad chose the settlement for its new headquarters and rail center. The railroad was planning a new, more direct route between Cincinnati and Atlanta, and it needed a place for crew changes and engine servicing. The passenger station was built first, in 1906. A veritable railroad complex followed: roundhouse, sand house, cinder pits, coal bins, oil house, machine shop, blacksmith shop, boiler shop, planing mill, cabinet shop, powerhouse, car repair shop, water tanks, a store, offices, freight depot, and nearly 20 tracks.

The L&N also built houses for its workers, and Etowah was truly a company town where everyone lived, breathed, and worked the railroad. At its peak, more than 2,000 men were employed by the L&N here.

Etowah and its railroad industry flourished until 1928, when the L&N started to replace its wooden railroad carts with steel ones. Two hundred shop men were laid off. In the same year, the L&N closed its headquarters in Etowah, moving them to Knoxville. By 1931, the workforce at Etowah had shrunk to just 80.

Over the succeeding decades, Etowah diversified, and people found other work. Passenger trains continued to run until 1968. CSX, the freight train company, still operates a terminal in Etowah.

There isn't much in the way of accommodations in Etowah, so look at nearby Athens for a comfortable bed-and-breakfast.

Sights

Etowah's downtown district faces Highway 411 and the railroad. The historic **Gem Theater** (700 S. Tennessee Ave./U.S. 441, www.gemplayers. com), built in 1927, has been renovated and is the home of the Gem Theater Players. For information about upcoming shows, contact the Etowah Arts Commission at 423/263-7608. They typically produce about five shows annually.

You can relive Etowah's railroad history at the **L&N Depot and Railroad Museum** (Tennessee Ave./Hwy. 411, 423/263-7840, Mon.–Sat. 10 A.M.–4 P.M., free). The old passenger station is elegant, with high ceilings and delicate wood finishes. It comes alive through old photographs and recollections by area residents who talk about the hardships and pleasures of a railroad life. The exhibit, called "Growing Up with the L&N: Life and Times of a Railroad Town," is more about the social history of Etowah than the railroad itself, although the two are interlinked.

Ask to go upstairs, where you can see more general exhibits about Etowah's history. Sometimes there are local art exhibits on display.

After touring the museum, go outside to see a railroad caboose. There is also a picnic area and a walking trail that follows the railroad tracks.

◀ Tennessee Valley Railroad Excursions

The Tennessee Valley Railroad (423/894-8028, www.tvrail.com), based in Chattanooga, organizes sightseeing tours of the Cherokee National Forest during the summer and fall. The **Hiwassee River Rail Adventure** (adults $34, children $24) is a 3.5-hour, 50-mile journey that follows the path of the Hiwassee River and includes the breathtaking corkscrew loop around Bald Mountain. The **Copperhill Special** (adults $52, children $35) follows the same route as the Hiwassee journey but adds an additional 40-mile trip and lunchtime layover in Copperhill. Passengers on either journey meet at the L&N Depot and Railroad Museum in Etowah and are bussed to nearby Gee Creek State Park, where they board the train. Train cars are comfortable, with big windows and air-conditioning.

The scenic train excursions are made possible by the combined efforts of the Tennessee Overhill Association and the Tennessee Valley Railroad Museum.

Food

Directly across Tennessee Avenue (otherwise known as Highway 411) from the L&N Depot is **Tony's Italian Restaurant** (718 Tennessee Ave., 423/263-1940, daily 11 A.M.–10 P.M., $5–8), which serves pasta, pizza, calzones, and Italian-style subs. There is a buffet at lunch and dinner that includes lasagna, pizza, salad, and other house specialties.

A short drive north on Tennessee Avenue will take you to **Hah-Hah's Deli and Coffee Shoppee** (235 Hwy. 411 N., 423/263-7914, Mon.–Fri. 9 A.M.–4 P.M., $5–6), which serves coffee, sandwiches, and ice cream.

Information

Contact the **Etowah Area Chamber of Commerce** (727 Tennessee Ave., 423/263-2228, www.etowahcoc.org), located in the L&N building next to the museum, for visitor information. The **Tennessee Overhill Heritage Association** (423/263-7232, www.tennesseeoverhill.com) is a regional tourism agency based in Etowah, with offices in the railroad depot.

The Tellico

The headwaters of the Tellico River are high atop the peaks of the Cherokee Forest. The stream, noted for fishing, flows down the mountain and along the scenic Cherohala Skyway to Tellico Plains, where it flows northward to its confluence with the Little Tennessee. The Tellico Dam impounds the rivers and forms Tellico Lake. Here, near the town of Vonore, are two of the most significant historic attractions in the region: Fort Loudoun State Historic Area and the Sequoyah Birthplace Museum. Both have important ties to Cherokee history.

Towns including Athens, Englewood, and Madisonville are located in the foothills of the mountains, in the Great Valley of East Tennessee. These centers of industry, education, and commerce are still the heartbeat of the Overhill region.

TELLICO PLAINS

Located where the Tellico River emerges from the national forest, Tellico Plains was once a logging and industrial town. It is now a gateway to the Cherokee National Forest and the official

beginning point of the Cherohala Skyway, a scenic parkway that extends into North Carolina.

The **Cherohala Skyway Visitor Center** (225 Cherohala Skyway/Hwy. 165, 423/253-8010, www.cherohala.org/visitorcenter.html, daily 9 A.M.–5 P.M.), near the official start of the skyway, has maps as well as staff to answer questions. There is also a large gift shop and bathrooms. Right next door is the **Charles Hall Museum** (229 Cherohala Skyway, 423/253-6767, www.charleshallmuseum.com, Mon.–Sat. 10 A.M.–5 P.M., Sun. noon–5 P.M., free), a local history museum packed with antiques, 98 percent of which came from the collection of Tellico-area resident Charles Hall. There are more than 200 guns, an extensive telephone collection, and an impressive coin collection, among others. In 2010 more than 30,000 people visited this small museum.

Tellico Plains consists of an older "downtown" located on the south side of Highway 165, and several miles of sprawl along Highway 68. The downtown area is home to several real estate offices, building supply companies, local businesses, restaurants, and shops. **Motorcycle Outfitters** (106 Scott St., 423/253-2088, www.tellicomoto.com) sells clothes and equipment for bikers, and **The Bookshelf** (108 Scott St., 423/253-3183, www.tellicobookshelf.com) is a used-book store with a knowledgeable staff that also repairs books. Galleries including **The Tellico Arts Center** (113 Scott St., 423/253-2253) cater to visitors looking for local arts and crafts.

For food, head first to **Tellico Grains Bakery** (105 Depot St., 423/253-6911, www.tellico-grains-bakery.com, Tues.–Sat. 8 A.M.–4 P.M., $4–8), a bakery and café with its own wood-fired oven. The menu of bread, sandwiches, and pizza are as clever as the bakery's name.

For plate lunches, burgers, and other grilled sandwiches, go to **Town Square Café and Bakery** (Public Sq., 423/253-2200, Mon.–Sat. 6 A.M.–7:30 P.M., Sun. 6 A.M.–3 P.M., $3–8), a cozy eating house where everyone seems to know each other. The daily lunch special comes with your choice of two sides and bread. They also sell pizza, but it is the homemade gravy on the breakfast dishes that brings in the locals.

Cherohala Skyway

Completed in 1996, this is a two-lane highway that passes through the highest peaks of the southern Unaka Mountains. The 54-mile road, which begins in Tellico Plains, climbs to more than 5,300 feet at its highest level and provides stunning scenic views. It follows the Tellico River for several miles at the beginning before starting its serious ascent. The road terminates in Robbinsville, North Carolina; about one-third of the road is in Tennessee.

The Cherohala Skyway was originally called the Cheoah Parkway and the Overhill Skyway; the states of Tennessee and North Carolina eventually agreed on the existing name, which combines the words *Cherokee* and *Nantahala*. The highway, which took

34 years and some $100 million to build, replaced narrow, unpaved Forest Service roads that had for many years been the only means of travel over the peaks in this part of the forest. Despite predictions to the contrary, the skyway remains relatively uncrowded, providing a pleasant alternative to congested highways through the Great Smoky Mountains National Park.

It will take you about 1.5 hours to drive nonstop from one end of the skyway to the other. Although the road is well maintained and easy to drive, plan to take it slow. It is windy, and you will want to stop frequently to admire the view. Beware of snow and ice during winter.

Sights and stops along the way include **Tellico Ranger Station** (250 Ranger Station Rd., 423/253-2520), a source of information about the forest, the area, and the drive. The station is located in a New Deal–era CCC building. **Bald River Falls**, a 100-foot waterfall, is located off the skyway along Forest Service Road 210.

After you pass the ranger station, the road begins to climb. Overlooks on the Tennessee side include **Turkey Creek, Lake View,** and **Brushy Ridge.** There are picnic tables at Turkey Creek and Brushy Ridge. All overlooks are wheelchair accessible.

The skyway is popular with motorcyclists and serious bicyclists who enjoy the scenic curves and fresh mountain air.

Indian Boundary

One of the most popular destinations in the southern Cherokee Forest, Indian Boundary (Forest Service Rd. 345, Apr.–Sept.) is a Forest Service campground and recreation area. Located high atop the mountains off the Cherohala Skyway, Indian Boundary is cool in the summer and an ideal place for a camping vacation. Cool off with a swim at the Indian Boundary beach, hike or bike along the three-mile loop that circles the 100-acre Indian

Boundary Lake, or go for a boat cruise on the lake. No gasoline engines are allowed in the lake.

The **campground** (877/444-6777, www.reserveusa.com, $20) has 91 sites, hot showers, and potable water available from spigots around the campground. Several sites have electricity. There is also a camp store (no phone) and picnic area. Despite Indian Boundary's isolation, it is quite popular, particularly during the summer. For information on recreation, contact the Tellico Ranger Station at 423/253-2520.

ENGLEWOOD

A small town located in the foothills of the Appalachian mountains, Englewood is home to the **Englewood Textile Museum** (17 S. Niota St., 423/887-5455, Tues.–Sat. noon–5 P.M., free). The museum remembers the hundreds of area working-class women who toiled at textile mills in Englewood. A hand-painted mural on the outside of the museum depicts a pastoral company town. Inside, you can see some of the clothing that was manufactured here for nearly 100 years. There is an adjacent antiques store.

Food

The ◖ **Tellico Junction Café** (17 Main St., 423/887-7770, Mon.–Fri. 6 A.M.–8 P.M., Sat. 7 A.M.–4 P.M., Sun. 7 A.M.–noon, $5–12) is a large, open restaurant facing the railroad tracks in downtown Englewood. Dozens of polished wood tables and a wide lunch counter invite you to stop and linger over cups of coffee or plates of grilled sandwiches, plate-lunch specials, or homemade dessert. Locals head here after church on Sunday or for fish fry on Friday. No matter when you come, don't miss the chance to check out the decor in the men's restroom.

ATHENS

The seat of McMinn County, Athens is home to **Tennessee Wesleyan University** (204 E. College St., 423/745-7504, www.twcnet.edu), a Methodist-affiliated four-year university.

Chartered in 1857, it is the home of the Old College Harp Singers, a shape-note singing group.

The **McMinn Living History Museum** (522 W. Madison Ave., 423/745-0329, Mon.–Fri. 10 A.M.–5 P.M., adults $5, students and seniors $3) is home to 30 different exhibit rooms, including an extensive collection of antique quilts.

One of the Southeast's most distinctive food brands is Mayfield, a maker of milk, dairy, and juice products. Mayfield's largest bottling and processing plant is located just outside of Athens, near where Thomas B. Mayfield Sr., a local dairy farmer, first opened his creamery in 1923. Visitors are welcome at **Mayfield Dairy Farms** (4 Mayfield Ln., 800/629-3435, www.mayfielddairy.com, Mon.–Fri. 9 A.M.–5 P.M., Sat. 9 A.M.–2 P.M., free). The 40-minute tour includes a short video and visits to viewing areas where you can see Mayfield's distinctive yellow milk jugs being made, jugs and other containers being filled, and ice cream being packaged. You also walk by giant vats of milk being pasteurized, and others that are being made into buttermilk. Milk is not made on Wednesday, and ice cream is not made on Saturday.

Don't expect to see any cows, though, except for the bronze cow sculpture outside the welcome center. Mayfield buys its raw milk from area dairy farmers; it arrives in giant trucks that enter the dairy gates by the dozens every day.

The tour is free, but be aware that it is awfully hard to pass up the ice cream shop at the end, particularly on a hot summer day. It's almost as if they planned it that way.

Accommodations

The **Majestic Mansion** (202 E. Washington Ave., 423/746-9041, www.themansionbnb.com, $115–145) is a bed-and-breakfast in downtown residential Athens. Four guest rooms offer classic country decor with elegant touches such as claw-foot tubs, feather beds, and polished brass fittings. Each room has a

Take an easy stroll to an underground lake at The Lost Sea Adventure.

private bath, air-conditioning, and television. For breakfast choose between "fitness fare" and "full power breakfast." Spend a quiet afternoon relaxing on the screened-in front porch or in the sitting room. In-room spa service is available at reasonable prices.

MADISONVILLE

Epicureans should make a beeline to **Benton's Country Hams** (2603 Hwy. 411, 423/442-5003), a family-run ham house where they depend on brown sugar, salt, and a lot of time to cure their hams. Housed in a low-slung inconspicuous cinderblock building on the side of busy Highway 411, Benton's has been a destination for cooks and eaters for generations. Their smoked and unsmoked country hams sell like hotcakes. You can also buy prosciutto, bacon, and luncheon meats that will have you dreaming pig. You know this is the real thing because the scent of hickory smoke clings to your clothes and hair after you depart.

SWEETWATER

The Lost Sea Adventure (140 Lost Sea Rd., 423/337-6616, www.thelostsea.com, Nov.–Feb. daily 9 A.M.–5 P.M., Mar.–Apr. and Sept.–Oct. daily 9 A.M.–6 P.M., May–June and Aug. daily 9 A.M.–7 P.M., July daily 9 A.M.–8 P.M., adults $16, children $8) is a cave noted for its four-acre underground lake. Tours include a 0.75-mile guided tour of the caverns, as well as a ride aboard a glass-bottomed boat on the lake. You can even sign up to camp out down in the cave in one of the Lost Sea's so-called wild tours. This is a memorable experience. The Lost Sea is located at exit 60 off I-75.

While in Sweetwater, satisfy your sweet tooth at **Hunter's Bakery and Café** (101 E. Morris St., 423/351-1098, www.huntersbakeryandcafe.com, Mon.–Thurs. 10 A.M.–4 P.M., Fri.–Sat. 9 A.M.–8 P.M., lunch $2–16, dinner $10–25). This cozy downtown hot spot has a fox-hunting theme and solidly good food that keeps people coming back again and again.

Boating, fishing, and history lessons come together at the Fort Loudoun State Historic Area.

Salads, pasta, and entrées including steak, pork, chicken, and shrimp are offered at lunch and dinner. At the midday meal, you can also pick from signature sandwiches like the tuna melt or the Reuben.

No matter how full you are after your meal, grab one of the café's home-baked big cookies or other confectionaries for the road.

VONORE

Two side-by-side historical attractions located on Tellico Lake focus on the state's Native American history, but from distinctly different eras and perspectives. Fort Loudoun State Historic Area marks the early era of contact between colonists and Cherokee Indians, while the Sequoyah Birthplace Museum looks in greater detail at the tribe's later interactions with white settlers, including its tragic removal via the Trail of Tears in 1838.

◖ Fort Loudoun State Historic Area

The Fort Loudoun State Historic Area (338 Fort Loudoun Rd., 423/884-6217, daily 8 A.M.–4:30 P.M., free) recalls the British fort that was built in this spot in 1756 to woo the Cherokee Indians during the French and Indian War. The war between the British and the French, and their respective Indian allies, was fought to decide which European power would control the new American colonies. The British built Fort Loudoun in an effort to cement its alliance with the Cherokee, and therefore strengthen their position to win the war against the French.

Fort Loudoun was located along the Little Tennessee River, and it was the very edge of the American frontier. At first, the British managed to maintain good relations with their Cherokee neighbors. But the uncertain alliance ultimately failed, and violence broke out, with each side blaming the other for the problems. After a five-month siege of Fort Loudoun in 1760, the British surrendered. The British negotiated the terms of their surrender with the Cherokee, who agreed to let the 180 men together with 60 women and children retreat to Charleston, South Carolina.

When the British party stopped to camp their first night, their Cherokee guides slipped into the forest, and by the next day some 29 of the Fort Loudoun party had been killed, including three women. While the basic facts of the ambush are clear, the motivation of the Cherokee is not. Their actions may have been in retribution for the earlier deaths of some 30 Cherokee at the hands of the British. Or they may have been angry that the British had buried the cannons and destroyed the gunpowder at the fort, contrary to the terms of the surrender.

Whatever the cause, it was a bloody and somber end to the Cherokee-British alliance in the Overhill Tennessee region.

Today, Fort Loudoun sits on the bank of

Tellico Lake. The last and most controversial of TVA's dam projects, Tellico Dam was finally closed in 1979 after nearly a decade of debate over its impact on the environment and the loss of historic Cherokee sites.

The park visitors center houses a good museum about the fort, and the film here is one of the best at a Tennessee state park. About 200 yards behind the visitors center is a replica of Fort Loudoun, built according to the archaeological evidence and contemporary accounts from the fort. The simple wooden buildings and the fort walls have been faithfully reconstructed. It is a pleasant place that conjures up the remoteness that would have existed in the 18th century, when the original fort was built.

Every September the **18th Century Trade Faire** depicts a colonial-era marketplace with merchants, artisans, and entertainers. At Christmas, there are candlelight tours of the fort. In addition, every month there are special programs that include costumed British soldiers and Cherokee Indians.

Fort Loudoun State Historic Area also has a picnic area, five miles of hiking trails, and fishing from a 50-foot pier that projects over Tellico Lake.

Sequoyah Birthplace Museum

Sequoyah was a Cherokee Indian born in about 1776 to Nathaniel Gist, a Virginia fur trader, and Wurteh, the daughter of a Cherokee chief. A silversmith by trade, Sequoyah is most famous for creating a written syllabary for the Cherokee language.

It was 1809 when Sequoyah first started to experiment with a written language for the Cherokee. During this period there was extensive interaction between white settlers and the Cherokee, and Sequoyah saw that a written language would allow his people to record their history, write letters, and communicate news.

Sequoyah developed the language independently, and his first student was his young daughter, Ayoka. Together, in 1821, Ayoka and Sequoyah introduced the language to Cherokee elders, and within a few months thousands of Cherokee were using the system of 85 symbols. By 1825 much of the Bible and numerous hymns had been translated, and in 1828 the *Cherokee Phoenix* became the first national bilingual newspaper in the country.

The story of Sequoyah's accomplishment and the broader legacy of the Cherokee people is preserved at the **Sequoyah Birthplace Museum** (Hwy. 360, 423/884-6246, www.sequoyahmuseum.org, Mon.–Sat. 9 A.M.–5 P.M., Sun. noon–5 P.M., adults $3, seniors $2.50, children 6–12 $1.50), a museum that is managed by the Eastern Band of the Cherokee.

Though dated, the museum provides a thorough and detailed rendering of the Cherokee way of life, the history of the tribe, and the story of Sequoyah himself. At the rear of the museum, at the end of a 100-yard gravel walkway, there is a mound where the remains of 221 Cherokee people are buried. The graves were moved here during the excavation that took place before Tellico Lake was formed.

Every September, the Sequoyah Birthplace Museum hosts a **Fall Festival,** featuring a Cherokee living-history camp, music, storytelling, Cherokee games, and dance.

Chota and Tanasi Memorials

The towns of Tanasi and Chota were the mother towns of the Overhill Cherokee. It is from the word *Tanasi* that the name Tennessee is derived. The Cherokee were forced to leave Tanasi, Chota, and other settlements as white settlers moved west into Tennessee, taking more and more Cherokee land.

When Tellico Lake was created in 1979, the sites of these historic Cherokee settlements were flooded. Before the inundation, University of Tennessee archaeologists explored the sites and found the remains of a great town house and the grave of the Cherokee warrior and chief Oconostota, who died in 1783.

After the lake was formed, the Tennessee Historical Commission erected a stone memorial that overlooks the actual site of Tanasi. The pavement in front of the marker is an octagonal slab representing a town house, and in the center of this is a granite marker engraved with a seven-pointed star, which represents the seven clans of the Cherokee.

One mile north of the Tanasi monument is the parking area for the Chota memorial. It is a quarter-mile walk from the parking area to the memorial, which consists of a full-scale replica of a Cherokee town house. The memorial, which stands on a raised surface built above the level of the lake, was erected by the Eastern Band of the Cherokee.

The Tanasi and Chota memorials are located off Bacon Ferry Road. To get there, take Highway 360 to Monroe County Road 455. After about six miles on Route 455, you will see the turnoff for Bacon Ferry Road and signs to the memorials. Both sites are also popular places for bird-watching.

KNOXVILLE

Perhaps Tennessee's most underappreciated city, Knoxville sits on the banks of the Tennessee River, in the foothills of the Appalachian Mountains. Knoxville lacks the immediate identity of other major Tennessee cities—it is not the birthplace of the blues, Music City USA, or the home of the Choo Choo. (Unless, of course, you are a college sports fan.) But that's okay with locals. Knoxville's viewpoint is ultimately an insular one—this is a city that does not strive to be. It just is.

And what is Knoxville? It is the gateway to the Smokies and the home of the orange-clad University of Tennessee Volunteers. It is an old industrial city with a long, rich history.

Whatever name you choose to put on Knoxville, dedicate some time to exploring it. The city skyline is dominated by the iconic gold-plated Sunsphere, built during the 1982 World's Fair. Along Gay Street and in the Old City downtown you will find restaurants, bars, and concert halls that are putting Knoxville on the musical map. The University of Tennessee campus is a hotbed of athletic and cultural events. In old suburbs scattered around the city you will find jewels in the rough, including the Knoxville Zoo, Beck Cultural Center, and Ijam's Nature Center.

Knoxville is a city without pretensions. It is a place that gets better the more you get to know it.

Within a half-hour drive from Knoxville are several must-see communities with their

HIGHLIGHTS

◖ The Sunsphere: Love it or hate it, the gold-plated globe of the Sunsphere defines the Knoxville skyline. Ride to the top for views of Knoxville and the surrounding area (page 60).

◖ WDVX Blue Plate Special: Almost every city in the state has a musical icon. Community radio station WDVX is it in Knoxville. It provides a live lunchtime concert every weekday at the Knoxville Visitor Center (page 69).

◖ Green McAdoo Cultural Center: The story of the desegregation of Clinton's high school is movingly presented at this multimedia museum (page 81).

◖ Museum of Appalachia: This museum pays tribute to the ingenuity, creativity, and tenacity of the mountain folk who settled in the southern Appalachian mountains (page 82).

◖ Oak Ridge National Laboratory: Get the behind-the-scenes look at what makes The Secret City tick when you tour this essential stop in atomic history (page 87).

LOOK FOR ◖ TO FIND RECOMMENDED SIGHTS, ACTIVITIES, DINING, AND LODGING.

own history and attractions. Oak Ridge is one of three places in the United States that built the components of the atomic bombs used at Hiroshima and Nagasaki, and it continues to be home to a nuclear facility. The glimpse of the United States you'll find here is unlike anything anywhere else in the United States. Sleepy Norris houses a remarkable museum about the Appalachian way of life, and Clinton is the site of a significant, but oft-overlooked, scene in the U.S. civil rights movement.

HISTORY

Knoxville's first settler was James White, who in 1786 built a fort where First Creek flows into the Tennessee River and named it after himself. In 1791 governor William Blount chose the fort as capital of the Territory South of the River Ohio and renamed it after secretary of war Henry Knox.

In the same year the first lots of land were sold, and the town of Knoxville was born. Street names were borrowed from Philadelphia and Baltimore, and four lots were reserved for Blount College, to be Knoxville's first school. Shortly after the town was laid out, Governor Blount built a frame house overlooking the river, which became the territorial capitol. Knoxville was incorporated in 1815.

During its first 50 years, Knoxville was primarily a way station for travelers making their

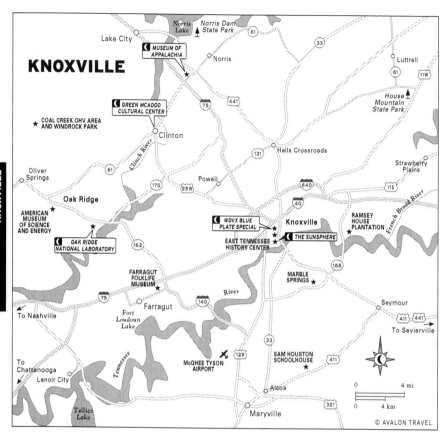

way along the Tennessee River or overland on stage roads. The population grew slowly to about 2,000 in 1850, and during the decade before the Civil War the number of residents more than doubled to about 5,000, thanks to the arrival of the East Tennessee and Georgia Railroad.

A majority of Knoxvillians voted to secede from the Union in the June 1861 referendum. But some city residents, and most East Tennesseans who lived in the rural countryside surrounding Knoxville, supported the Union. Initially Knoxville was occupied by the Confederate Army under Gen. Felix Zollicoffer, whose job was to keep the rail lines open. After East Tennessee Unionists started to harass the Southern troops and burn up railroad bridges, General Zollicoffer launched a campaign of repression against Union supporters in the city and surrounding areas.

Zollicoffer's troops were called south to fight in the fall of 1863, and Federal troops under the command of Gen. Ambrose Burnside quickly took Knoxville. Burnside built a series of forts around the city, which enabled him to easily repulse an attempted attack by Confederates under command of Gen. James Longstreet in November 1863. Knoxville remained under Union control for the duration of the war. Union supporters returned to the city and retaliated against the Confederate sympathizers who had had the upper hand during the early period of the war.

After the Civil War, Knoxville experienced an industrial expansion. Iron and cloth mills, machine shops, apparel and furniture factories, and marble quarries were built. Thanks to the railroad, the city was a major distribution center; in 1896 Knoxville was the third-largest wholesale center in the South, behind Atlanta and New Orleans.

During this time, the first suburbs developed. West Knoxville, now called Fort Sanders, became the city's premier residential area, with many fine homes and mansions built around the turn of the 20th century. With prosperity came people; by 1900 Knoxville had a population of 32,637.

Like any city, Knoxville was not without problems. Pollution from factories made the city air and water unhealthy. Race relations were strained, and African Americans were stripped of power by political gerrymandering and economic discrimination. As urban problems grew, the city's elite moved into suburbs farther and farther from the city center.

Events in 1919 showed the tensions of the day. In August of that year, a riotous white mob tore down the city jail in search of a mixed-race man who had been charged with murdering a white woman. When the mob did not find the suspect, Maurice Mayes, they headed to the black section of town to cause havoc. When the dust settled, one National Guard officer and one African American had been killed. Thirty-six white men were arrested for their actions, but an all-white jury refused to convict. It was a different story for Maurice Mayes, who was convicted and eventually executed for murder.

During the mid-20th century the trend of outward expansion continued in Knoxville. From the 1950s to the 1980s, Knoxville's downtown deteriorated as retail shops closed and people moved to the suburbs. Central Knoxville became a no-man's-land where only downtown office workers dared to venture.

In the early 1980s, Knoxville was famously dubbed "a scruffy little city."

Some people trace the present downtown renaissance to the 1982 World's Fair, when the Sunsphere and the World's Fair Park were built and 11 million people came to visit the internationally themed festival event. *Time* magazine uncharitably dubbed the event "Barn Burner in a Backwater," and the *Philadelphia Inquirer* said the grounds were built along a wasted gully of Second Creek, a place that was "like a hole in your sock."

Despite the fears that the World's Fair was overly ambitious, it did break even financially and left Knoxville with a park that the city—some 20 years later—finally decided to use to its full advantage. Over the succeeding years, downtown Knoxville has staged a comeback, with the addition of a downtown art museum, the birth of an entertainment district in the Old City, and, most recently, the rebirth of Gay Street and Market Square as centers for business, commerce, and residential living.

PLANNING YOUR TIME

Knoxville is an ideal destination for a long weekend: Spend a day exploring downtown attractions around Gay Street and the World's Fair Park, and then choose two destinations outside of town—such as the Museum of Appalachia, Oak Ridge, or Clinton—for your second and third days. For the best atmosphere, find a hotel within walking distance of Gay Street and the Old City so you can walk to restaurants and music venues.

Whatever you do, don't plan your trip to coincide with a University of Tennessee home football game, unless that's your purpose for coming to town.

ORIENTATION

Knoxville lies on the shore of the Tennessee River, also called Fort Loudoun Lake. The original city and today's downtown center sit atop a bluff overlooking the river. The main thoroughfares through downtown are **Gay**

Street, with its delightful historic storefronts, and **Henley Street,** which becomes Chapman Highway to the south and Broadway to the north. The Henley Street and Gay Street bridges are the primary routes over the Tennessee River.

Immediately west of downtown is the **World's Fair Park,** identifiable by the gold-plated Sunsphere. The **University of Tennessee** and one of the city's first suburbs, **Fort Sanders,** lie just west of the World's Fair park. Cumberland Avenue, also known as "The Strip," is the university's main drag, and it divides UT from Fort Sanders. In recent years, many beautiful old historic homes in Fort Sanders have been torn down for the construction of condominiums.

Cumberland Avenue turns into Kingston Pike, which heads westward from UT, passing suburbs of progressive vintage, beginning with **Sequoyah Hills** and **Bearden.** This land of shopping malls, traffic jams, and sprawl is now called **West Knoxville.**

There are several pleasant historic neighborhoods north and east of the city center. **Fourth and Gill** lies north of town near Emory Place, once a commercial center at the northern end of Gay Street. **Mechanicsville,** north of Western Avenue, developed as housing near Knoxville's old industrial center and is now anchored by Knoxville College. Magnolia Avenue was the primary thoroughfare headed eastward, to neighborhoods including **Park City** and **Holston Hills.**

Sights

DOWNTOWN

Downtown Knoxville lies east of Henley Street and includes the oldest areas of the city, plus its modern-day commercial and government center.

East Tennessee History Center

There is an excellent museum about the history of East Tennessee at the East Tennessee History Center (601 S. Gay St., 865/215-8824, www.easttnhistory.org, Mon.–Fri. 9 A.M.–4 P.M., Sat. 10 A.M.–4 P.M., Sun. 1–5 P.M., free). The permanent exhibit, titled "Voices of the Land: The People of East Tennessee," offers a sweeping survey of East Tennessee history, from its early Native American inhabitants to the beginnings of the modern-day tourist trade in the Great Smoky Mountains. In between, you learn about the region's groundbreaking abolitionists, its writers and musicians, and the everyday lives of residents during tumultuous periods like the Civil War and the civil rights movement. The voices of more than 350 people are used to bring the tale to life, as are artifacts

such as Davy Crockett's rifle, a ring once belonging to Cherokee "Beloved Woman" Nancy Ward, and the painting *Hauling of Marble* by Lloyd Branson. The underlying message is that East Tennessee's story cannot be lumped into that of the entire state; the region is unique.

The exhibit includes several audio and video presentations, and hundreds of panels to read and examine. Plan on spending at least two hours here.

The history center is located in the city's old customs house, a handsome white marble structure built in 1874. For most of its life, the building housed federal offices and a U.S. post office. Later, it was a headquarters for the Tennessee Valley Authority.

James White Fort

The oldest home in Knoxville is found at James White Fort (205 E. Hill Ave., 865/525-6514, www.jameswhitesfort.org, Apr.–Nov. Mon.–Sat. 9:30 A.M.–5 P.M., closed during UT home football games, Dec.–Mar. Mon.–Fri. 10 A.M.–4 P.M., adults $7, children 5–17 $3).

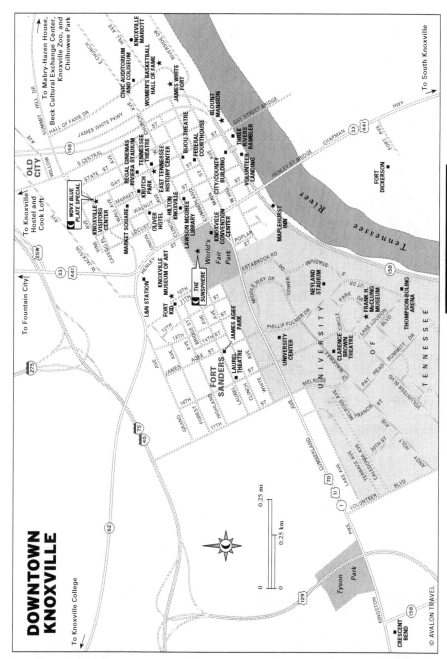

KNOXVILLE

DOWNTOWN KNOXVILLE

To Knoxville College

To Fountain City

To Knoxville Hostel and Cook Loft

OLD CITY

To Mabry-Hazen House, Beck Cultural Exchange Center, Knoxville Zoo, and Chilhowee Park

To South Knoxville

CIVIC AUDITORIUM AND COLISEUM

KNOXVILLE MARRIOTT

WOMEN'S BASKETBALL HALL OF FAME

JAMES WHITE FORT

BLOUNT MANSION

THREE RIVERS RAMBLER

BIJOU THEATRE

FEDERAL COURTHOUSE

TENNESSEE THEATRE

REGAL CINEMAS RIVIERA STADIUM

EAST TENNESSEE HISTORY CENTER

CITY/COUNTY BUILDING

VOLUNTEER LANDING

WDVX BLUE PLATE SPECIAL

KNOXVILLE VISITORS CENTER

MARKET SQUARE

KRUTCH PARK

OLIVER HOTEL

HILTON KNOXVILLE

LAWSON MCGHEE LIBRARY

KNOXVILLE CONVENTION CENTER

MAPLEHURST INN

FORT DICKERSON

Tennessee River

World's Fair Park

L&N STATION

KNOXVILLE MUSEUM OF ART

FORT KID

THE SUNSPHERE

ESTABROOK RD

NEYLAND STADIUM

FRANK H. McCLUNG MUSEUM

THOMPSON-BOLING ARENA

UNIVERSITY CENTER

CLARENCE BROWN THEATRE

JAMES AGEE PARK

LAUREL THEATRE

FORT SANDERS

UNIVERSITY OF TENNESSEE

CRESCENT BEND

Tyson Park

0   0.25 mi

0   0.25 km

© AVALON TRAVEL

East Tennessee History Center

Gen. James White acquired more than 1,000 acres of land in 1783 under the so-called Land Grab Act passed by the North Carolina legislature. White and his wife, Mary Lawson, moved to the frontier in 1785 and constructed a log cabin near the junction of the French Broad and Holston Rivers, to the west of First Creek. Soon, White built additional log structures and protected them with a stockade; he called the place James White's Fort. Later, William Blount chose the location as the first capital of the Southwest Territory and renamed the fort Knoxville.

White hired Charles McClung to survey his 1,000 acres, and in 1791 he sold lots in the new city of Knoxville for $8 each. White donated lots for a town common, church, and cemetery, and he sold lots for Blount College for a nominal amount.

As Knoxville grew, White's rough-hewn log cabin was threatened by development. In 1906 a local citizen, Isaiah Ford, bought the fort and carefully moved the structures to a site on Woodland Avenue. In 1960, the fort was moved again to its present location on Hill Avenue. Visitors will learn about White, the establishment of Knoxville, and the rugged way of life on the Tennessee frontier.

Blount Mansion

The Blount Mansion (200 W. Hill Ave., 865/525-2375, www.blountmansion.org, summer Tues.–Sat. 9:30 A.M.–5 P.M., Oct.–May Tues.–Sat. 10 A.M.–5 P.M., adults $7, seniors $6, children 6–17 and students $5) is Knoxville's best historic attraction. First built between 1792 and 1796 by territorial governor William Blount, the "mansion" underwent no fewer than six periods of construction and alteration during its lifetime. The original structure was the first frame home in Knoxville and one of the first in the whole state. The Cherokee called Blount's home the House with Many Glass Eyes because of its large glass windows.

Significant events in Tennessee history took place at Blount Mansion. It is believed that it

THE CRADLE OF COUNTRY MUSIC

Knoxville's place in country music history is not as well known as that of Memphis or Nashville, but the roots of several seminal country artists are buried deep in Knoxville history. Several Knoxville institutions are also closely linked with the emergence of country music on the national stage.

The **Andrew Johnson Hotel** (912 S. Gay St.) is now a government office building, but for many years it was Knoxville's landmark hotel. WNOX broadcast the live *Midday Merry-Go-Round* from the hotel, and in 1952, Hank Williams checked in on what would be the final day of his life. It is still a matter of discussion whether Williams was alive when his teenage chauffeur put him in the backseat of a Cadillac and drove north for a gig in Canton, Ohio. During a pit stop in Oak Hill, West Virginia, the driver discovered that Williams was dead; he was just 29 years old.

In 1932 the **Tennessee Theatre** (604 S. Gay St.) hosted the first public performance by Union County native Roy Acuff, who performed in a talent contest with his band, Three Rolling Stones.

Knoxville has memorialized its musical history at the **Knoxville Music Monument** (Gay St. and Summit Hill Dr.), which features likenesses of Chet Atkins, an East Tennessee native later known as Mr. Guitar; Archie Campbell, a country music comedian and radio host from nearby Bulls Gap; and Unknown Musicians, representative of jazz, blues, country, and rock 'n' roll artists whose contributions have gone largely unwritten.

It was from a storefront on **Market Square** that Sam Morrison of Bell Sales Company promoted Elvis Presley's "That's All Right (Mama)" by playing it on a loudspeaker outside. Morrison sold hundreds of copies of the single, including two to an RCA talent scout. Several months later, RCA bought Presley's recording contract from Sun Studio in Memphis.

For a detailed tour of Knoxville music history, follow the Cradle of Country Music Walking Tour. A printed guide is available from the Knoxville Visitor Center (301 S. Gay St., 865/523-7263, www.knoxville.org).

was here that governor William Blount wrote the first Tennessee constitution. The mansion also served as the second territorial capitol of the soon-to-be state.

Blount Mansion consists today of restored living quarters, office, kitchen, and gardens, as well as a visitors center that houses exhibits about Blount and his home. Guided tours depart at the top of every hour.

Market Square

Knoxville's old Market Square has been given new life thanks to downtown redevelopment over the past 20 years. Once a dirty and depressing corner of the city, Market Square is alive again with commerce. Restaurants, boutiques, and nightclubs populate the square. It is the venue for the city's farmers market on Saturday and Wednesday during the summer, and it is a popular location for outdoor events and concerts.

Come here to people-watch or to soak up some of Knoxville's youthful downtown vibe.

Find Market Square near the intersection of Market Street and Union Avenue, just a few blocks behind Gay Street. It is within easy walking distance of downtown attractions.

Women's Basketball Hall of Fame

In 1892, one year after James Naismith invented basketball, a woman coach introduced the sport at Smith College. The female sport underwent countless changes during its 100-plus-year history. A few of them: In 1918 bounce passes were legalized, in 1926 the first national women's collegiate championship was held, in 1962 players were permitted to "snatch" the ball from each other, and in 1976 women's basketball made its Olympic debut.

These and many other milestones are remembered at the Women's Basketball Hall of Fame

(700 Hall of Fame Dr., 865/633-9000, www. wbhof.com, summer Mon.–Sat. 10 A.M.–5 P.M., Sept.–Apr. Tues.–Fri. 11 A.M.–5 P.M., Sat. 10 A.M.–5 P.M., adults $7.95, seniors and children 6–15 $5.95), a museum dedicated to celebrating women's achievement on the basketball court and to fostering future talent.

The hall of fame consists of interactive exhibits that recall the history and development of women's basketball. Visitors will hear women's basketball "inventor" Senda Berenson share her thoughts on the early days of the game. They will sit in a modern-day locker room and hear half-time talks by some of the best coaches in the modern sport. This is not just a spectator museum. Downstairs are basketball courts where you can test your skill against the sport's best, shoot into baskets from different eras in history, and try on old and new uniforms. In addition, there are exhibits about international women's basketball, the WNBA, and top women's basketball college programs. Finally, visitors can pay tribute to the sport's best at the 127-member hall of fame.

The Women's Basketball Hall of Fame is located in an eye-catching building near the eastern end of Knoxville's waterfront. It is home to the world's largest basketball—30 feet tall and 10 tons heavy—which protrudes from the roof.

The hall of fame opened in Knoxville in 1999, and there was really no better city for it. The Tennessee Lady Vols are one of the most successful women's basketball teams in the country. Their former coach, Pat Summit, was renowned for style and success. Current coach Holly Warlick worked with the legendary Summitt, first as a player, then as an assistant and associate head coach. Summitt is the all-time winningest coach in men's or women's collegiate basketball, and Warlick was there for 922 of the 1071 wins collected by her mentor.

Volunteer Landing

A one-mile city park sits along the bank of the Tennessee River, providing a nice place to walk or bring the family.

At the eastern end of the park there is a playground and a statue symbolizing the Treaty of the Holston, which took the land on which Knoxville sits away from the Cherokee. This is where Tennessee riverboats depart.

Farther west is another playground and a series of fountains, perfect for romping around in on a hot summer day.

There are several commercial marinas and restaurants along the park. The best way to get here is to take the pedestrian bridge over Neyland Drive, which departs from the southwestern corner of the Knoxville City/County Building along Walnut Street.

WORLD'S FAIR PARK

Lying between the University of Tennessee and downtown is the grassy, pleasant grounds of the World's Fair Park. There are several reasons for visitors to head to this area.

◖ The Sunsphere

Knoxville's foremost landmark is the Sunsphere (World's Fair Park, Apr.–Oct. daily 9 A.M.–10 P.M., Nov.–Mar. daily 11 A.M.–6 P.M., free). Built for the 1982 World's Fair, the Sunsphere has been both a source of pride and consternation for Knoxvillians in years since. The Sunsphere, symbolic of the World's Fair theme "Energy Turns the World," is 266 feet tall. It consists of a five-story golden sphere—which the *New York Times* described as similar to a gold golf ball—perched atop a steel shaft. During the World's Fair, it housed two restaurants.

After the World's Fair ended, Knoxville couldn't decide what to do with the odd monument. Ideas came and went—restaurants, advertising billboard, visitors center—but from 1999 until 2007 the sphere was essentially closed all together. Around the 20th anniversary of the World's Fair, the city began to think again about what it could do with this iconic

The Sunsphere was built for the 1982 World's Fair.

landmark, and five years and $280,000 later, in time for the 25th anniversary of the fair, the city reopened the observation deck to visitors.

The observation deck is located on the 4th floor of the Sunsphere. After a long and clanky elevator ride up, you are deposited in a narrow circular room with a 360-degree view of Knoxville. It is a pretty neat view, and it puts the city in perspective. The Tennessee River sweeps southward, the University of Tennessee sits on the river bluff, and the interstate highways slice this way and that. You look right down on the World's Fair Park, and it's like seeing the world in miniature.

Panels around the observation deck tell about some of Knoxville's attractions and history, and there is a running video with footage from the 1982 World's Fair.

Other floors in the Sunsphere are rented by local businesses.

Knoxville Museum of Art

Located in a building faced dramatically with white marble and designed by New York architect Edward Larabee Barnes, the Knoxville Museum of Art (1050 World's Fair Park Dr., 865/525-6101, www.knoxart.org, Tues.–Sat. 10 A.M.–5 P.M., Sun. 1–5 P.M., free) is Knoxville's preeminent visual arts institution. Originally called the Dulin Gallery of Art and located in an early-20th-century mansion, the Knoxville Museum of Art moved to the World's Fair Park after the 1982 World's Fair. The current structure opened in 1990.

The museum has five galleries, an outdoor sculpture garden, gift shop, and an interactive exploratory gallery for children. From the rear of the great hall, visitors can step outside on the museum balcony for views of the World's Fair Park and downtown Knoxville. The museum's growing permanent collection is bolstered by numerous visiting exhibitions. On Friday evening the museum hosts Alive After Five, with jazz performances.

UNIVERSITY OF TENNESSEE

The preeminent public university in Tennessee, the University of Tennessee was founded in 1784 as Blount College. Originally centered at "the hill" on the eastern end of Cumberland Avenue, UT has spread out along the entire length of Cumberland. Its colors—orange and white—were inspired by the orange and white daisies that grow outside on the hill. UT has a student enrollment of more than 21,000.

At UT, it is athletics that are truly center stage, or at least so it seems. Take, for example, the fact that in recent years UT has renamed two major roads throughout the campus not after prizewinning scientists or writers, but after Peyton Manning, the UT quarterback who went on to take the Indianapolis Colts to the Super Bowl (and now plays for the Denver Broncos), and Phillip Fulmer, UT football's former head coach.

KNOXVILLE

Frank H. McClung Museum

The best all-around museum in Knoxville, the Frank H. McClung Museum (1327 Circle Park Dr., 865/974-2144, http://mcclungmuseum.utk.edu, Mon.–Sat. 9 A.M.–5 P.M., Sun. 1–5 P.M., free) houses a wide variety of historical, cultural, and natural-history exhibits. Longstanding exhibits explore ancient Egypt, the native peoples of Tennessee, and the Civil War in Knoxville. Other exhibits look at Tennessee's freshwater mussels and decorative arts in the state. The museum also hosts special temporary exhibits.

Ewing Gallery

UT's art museum is the Ewing Gallery (1715 Volunteer Blvd., 865/974-3200, www.ewing-gallery.utk.edu, Mon.–Fri. 10 A.M.–5 P.M., during the school year also on Sun. 1–4 P.M., free). Located on the first floor of the university's Art and Architecture Building, the Ewing Gallery is named for the founder of UT's art program. Student and faculty art share the 3,000-square-foot exhibition space with visiting shows from other museums.

Fort Sanders

Knoxville's original suburb, Fort Sanders is a quickly disappearing historic neighborhood that lies between the World's Fair Park and UT. The site of an earthen fort named for Gen. William Sanders, who died in the Battle of Knoxville in 1863, Fort Sanders was developed into a residential area beginning in the 1880s. This was home to Knoxville's upper-class merchants, mayors, university professors, and other persons of note. Author James Agee was raised in Fort Sanders.

Because of its vintage and the relative affluence of its residents, Fort Sanders's homes are lovely examples of American Victorian and early-20th-century architecture. Towers, broad porches, colorful shutters, and intricate detail work set Fort Sanders homes apart.

As the university grew, Fort Sanders was encroached. By the 1970s, many owners stopped occupying their homes and instead rented them to students. Homes deteriorated. During the 1990s and early years of this century, development has taken a great toll on Fort Sanders. In 1999 alone, 15 historic homes were razed to make room for condominium developments. The destruction caused an outcry, and some of Fort Sanders's historic homes are now protected from development.

You can see what is left of Fort Sanders along Highland, Laurel, Forest, and Grand Avenues, between 11th and 17th Streets. In 2009, the City of Knoxville and the Metropolitan Planning Commission began work on developing a long-range plan for sustainable development. A historical district was created, so steps are being taken to save this neighborhood and enhance its beauty. **James Agee Park,** at the corner of James Agee Street and Laurel Avenue, is located near the site of Agee's childhood home, where parts of Agee's Pulitzer Prize–winning work *A Death in the Family* are set.

WEST KNOXVILLE

Kingston Pike is the thoroughfare that connects downtown Knoxville with its western suburbs. Immediately past the University of Tennessee, Kingston Pike passes several historic homes. Farther west, you reach the communities of Bearden, West Hills, and Farragut.

Crescent Bend

The Armstrong-Lockett House, also called the romantic-sounding Crescent Bend (2728 Kingston Pk., 865/637-3163, www.crescentbend.com, Wed.–Fri. 10 A.M.–4 P.M., Sat. 10 A.M.–2 P.M., adults $7, students $5, children 12 and under free), was built in 1834 by Drury Paine Armstrong, a local merchant and public official. The brick farmhouse was once the centerpiece of a 600-acre farm. Now it consists of the elegant home and formal Italian gardens facing the Tennessee River.

Visitors who take the guided tour will see a fine collection of china, silver, and other antiques, including wallpaper originally meant for the Hermitage, President Andrew Jackson's home near Nashville.

During March and April Crescent Bend celebrates spring with Tuliptime. This is a delightful time to visit, when more than 20,000 tulips are in bloom. During Tuliptime, the home schedules candlelight dinners, high teas, and other special events.

Bleak House

Knoxville's Confederate Memorial Hall, better known as Bleak House (3148 Kingston Pk., 865/522-2371, www.knoxvillecmh.org, Wed.– Fri. 1–4 P.M., adults $5, seniors $4, discount for students and children, call first as hours are subject to change) was Gen. James Longstreet's headquarters during the Battle of Fort Sanders and other Civil War battles that took place November–December 1863. Built in 1858 for Robert Houston and Louisa Armstrong, the Italian villa–style home was named after the popular Charles Dickens novel of the day.

Visitors may be given a tour, which includes the tower where, legend has it, Confederate sharpshooters were stationed during the Civil War. There is a museum that includes Confederate artifacts.

Girl Scout Museum

Whether you have a sash of badges in the basement or just like the cookies, you'll want to make a stop here. East Tennessee's Girl Scout Council operates the Girl Scout Museum at Daisy's Place (1567 Downtown West Blvd., 865/688-9440, www.girlscoutcsa.org/about/ museums-2, Mon. 8:30 A.M.–7 P.M., Tues.–Fri. 8:30 A.M.–4:30 P.M., free). The museum, one of six such Girl Scout museums in the United States, features exhibits about the history of Girl Scouting, Girl Scout cookies, and scouting in East Tennessee. You can see handbooks,

songbooks, vintage uniforms, and scrapbooks dating back to 1912. There are lots of hands-on exhibits to experience. Bring a pin or trinket from your troop to swap for another.

Farragut Folklife Museum

The first U.S. admiral, David Glasgow Farragut, was born west of Knoxville in an area called Stoney Point. The family moved to New Orleans when Farragut was just five years old. When his mother died of yellow fever, Farragut was adopted by David Porter and moved to Chester, Pennsylvania. Farragut, who was born James Glasgow Farragut, changed his name to David in honor of his patron and entered the U.S. navy. His naval career was long and proud; Farragut's military service during the Civil War led to his promotion in 1866 to the rank of admiral. It was during an August 1864 battle aboard the USS *Hartford* when Farragut reportedly said, "Damn the torpedoes, full speed ahead," a phrase that lives on today.

The town that now exists near Admiral Farragut's birthplace took his name, and now the Farragut City Hall houses a museum dedicated to this mostly unknown Tennessean. The Farragut Folklife Museum (11408 Municipal Center Dr., Farragut, 865/966-7057, www. townoffarragut.org, Mon.–Fri. 10 A.M.– 4:30 P.M., free) also houses exhibits about the local marble industry, the Battle of Campbell's Station, and arts, crafts, and other memorabilia from the communities of Farragut and Concord.

Farragut is located near the intersection of Kingston Pike and Campbell Station Road, off I-40 exit 373.

EAST KNOXVILLE

Magnolia Avenue (U.S. 25 West) and Martin Luther King Boulevard are two thoroughfares that head east from downtown Knoxville. Originally a series of quiet residential neighborhoods, East Knoxville has gradually evolved into a mixture of low-rise office buildings, modest sprawl, and historic homes.

Mabry-Hazen House Museum

The Mabry-Hazen House Museum (1711 Dandridge Ave., 865/522-8661, www.mabry-hazen.com, Wed.–Fri. 11 A.M.–5 P.M., Sat. 10 A.M.–3 P.M., adults $5, students K–12 $2.50) is located on a pleasant rise in East Knoxville. This handsome home, with green shutters and a wide porch, housed three generations of the same family from 1858 to 1987 and served as headquarters for both Confederate and Union troops during the Civil War. Since 1992 it has been open to the public for tours. The Mabry name comes from Joseph Alexander Mabry Jr., a businessman who donated the land for Market Square and owned the *Knoxville Whig* from 1869 to 1870. The murders of Mabry and his son on Gay Street in 1882 were documented in Mark Twain's *Life on the Mississippi*. Mabry's daughter, Alice Mabry, married Rush Strong Hazen, a wealthy businessman. The third generation to live in the house was Evelyn Montgomery Hazen, who helped author the *Harbrace College Handbook,* a reference guide used by generations of English students.

Because staff at the home is limited, the house sometimes closes for appointments or tours of the nearby **Bethel Civil War Cemetery Museum** (1711 Dandridge Ave., Wed.–Fri. 11 A.M.–5 P.M., Sat. 10 A.M.–3 P.M.). Call the museum director at 865/951-6614 if you arrive and find no tour guide. Your wait until one arrives may be just a few minutes.

Beck Cultural Exchange Center

Knoxville's foremost African American historical and cultural center is the Beck Cultural Exchange Center (1927 Dandridge Ave., 865/524-8461, www.beckcenter.net, Tues.–Sat. 10 A.M.–6 P.M., free). Founded in 1975, Beck is a museum, education center, archive, and community gathering place. In addition to putting on a variety of programs throughout the year, Beck also welcomes visitors who want to learn more about Knoxville's African American history.

Among Beck's permanent exhibits is the William H. Hastie Room, dedicated to preserving the memory of the Knoxville native who became the first black governor of the U.S. Virgin Islands in 1946 and the first African American federal judge in the United States four years later. Beck also features a gallery with photographs and biographies of prominent African Americans from Knoxville.

The center also preserves the history of the struggle to desegregate Knoxville's public schools, the University of Tennessee, and Maryville College. There is also information about the historic desegregation of schools in Clinton, Tennessee, and the legacy of Austin High School, Knoxville's onetime all-black secondary school.

Alex Haley Square

Pulitzer Prize–winning author Alex Haley has roots in both East and West Tennessee. He grew up in Henning, a sawmill town along the Mississippi River, but he spent a great deal of his adult life in East Tennessee, giving both regions a claim to his legacy.

Haley's preeminence—but also his disarming and loving nature—is evident in a larger-than-life statue of the writer at Alex Haley Square (1600 Dandridge Ave.) in East Knoxville. In the figure, Haley is reading a book, seeming to invite the viewer to gather round and listen to a story. The statue, park, and playground opened in 1998, six years after Haley's death.

Knoxville Zoo

Children and adults alike love the Knoxville Zoo (3500 Knoxville Zoo Dr., 865/637-5331, www.knoxville-zoo.org, summer daily 9:30 A.M.–6 P.M., winter daily 10 A.M.–4:30 P.M., adults $19.95, seniors 65-plus and children 2–12 $15.95). More than 800 species of animals live at the zoo, in habitats including Grassland Africa, the Red Panda Village, and penguin pool. Giraffes, elephants, camels, giant tortoise, and gorillas are just a few of the iconic animals you will see at the zoo.

Attractions include a petting zoo, camel rides ($5), a colorful carousel ($2), and a Komodo dragon named Khaleesi.

Surrounding the zoo is Chilhowee Park, with picnic tables, walking paths, and a lake. Parking at the zoo costs $5 per vehicle.

East Tennessee Science Discovery Center

Also located at Chilhowee Park is the East Tennessee Science Discovery Center (Chilhowee Park, 865/594-1494, www.etdiscovery.org, Mon.–Fri. 9 A.M.–5 P.M., Sat. 10 A.M.–5 P.M., adults $4, seniors and children 5–18 $3, children 3–4 $2), an interactive children's museum. Exhibits include aquariums, whisper dishes, a replica space shuttle, and a liquid-crystal wall. There is also a planetarium; shows are offered most days at 2 and 4 P.M.

SOUTH KNOXVILLE

Chapman Highway (U.S. 441) begins south of the Henley Street Bridge and brings you to South Knoxville.

Ijams Nature Center

Knoxville's best outdoor attraction is Ijams Nature Center (2915 Island Home Ave., 865/577-4717, www.ijams.org, visitors center Mon.–Sat. 9 A.M.–5 P.M., grounds daily 8 A.M.–dusk, free). The visitors center is a modern earth-friendly construction that houses exhibits about lost animal species and the Ijams family. There is also an enclosure with a red-tailed hawk and a turkey vulture, plus native plant and animal species.

The real attraction at Ijams is the 160 acres of protected woodlands and meadows. Come here for a walk through the woods or a stroll along the Tennessee River boardwalk. The grounds also include the Ijams family historic homesite and Mead's Quarry. In total, there are seven miles of walking trails.

Ijams offers a regular schedule of special events: workshops, talks, guided walks, and fairs. Check the website for details.

Fort Dickerson

A Civil War–era earthen fort and three replica cannons are the historical attractions at the Knoxville city park on the south side of the Tennessee River. Panels explain the fort's significance during the battles of Knoxville that took place in the fall of 1863.

Visitors will also enjoy the view (particularly during the fall and winter, when the trees have shed their leaves) of the Knoxville skyline and the view of an old quarry.

Fort Dickerson Park is located three-quarters of a mile south of the Henley Street Bridge on Chapman Highway (U.S. 441). Look for the signs on your right.

Ramsey House Plantation

The home called "the most costly and most admired building in Tennessee" by the 1800 census taker is open for public tours in the 21st century. Ramsey House Plantation (2614 Thorngrove Pk., 865/546-0745, www.ramseyhouse.org, Wed.–Sat. 10 A.M.–4 P.M., adults $7, children 6–12 $5) was built between 1795 and 1797 by master carpenter and cabinetmaker Thomas Hope for Col. Francis Alexander Ramsey. Built in the late Georgian style out of pink marble, Ramsey House features intricately carved consoles and other distinctive decorative features. It was said to be the first stone house in Tennessee, as well as the first home in the state with an attached kitchen.

The site of the house is near the fork of the Holston and French Broad Rivers. It was close to a site called Swan Pond, a beaver dam pond well-known by hunters and travelers. Col. Ramsey drained the pond to create pasture and farmland.

Ramsey House was the home of Colonel Ramsey's son, James G. M. Ramsey, a doctor, businessman, and author of an authoritative early history of Tennessee, *The Annals of*

© BRIAN STANSBERRY/CREATIVE COMMONS

Old Gray Cemetery

Tennessee to the End of the Eighteenth Century. James Ramsey and his wife, Margaret Crozier, raised 11 children at the home, then called Mecklenburg. Ramsey supported the Confederate cause during the Civil War, and Mecklenburg was burned by Union troops during the war, destroying a valuable library and collection of early Tennessee antiquities. During the war years and until the early 1870s, Ramsey and his family lived in Atlanta, Savannah, and North Carolina. He returned to East Tennessee in the 1870s and remained here until his death in 1884.

Ramsey House was purchased in 1952 by the Association for the Preservation of Tennessee Antiquities. It has been fully restored and is open for tours, which include all rooms of the house, the kitchen, and the grounds. Ramsey House has a nice garden where heirloom vegetables and other plants are grown.

Ramsey House is located off Gov. John Sevier Highway southeast of downtown. The easiest way to get there from downtown is to take Chapman Highway (U.S. 441) south out of town. Turn left onto John Sevier Highway (Highway 168). After crossing the Tennessee River, look for Thorngrove Pike on your right and signs to Ramsey House.

Marble Springs

The early home of Tennessee's first governor, John Sevier, is preserved at Marble Springs (1220 John Sevier Hwy., 865/573-5508, www.marblesprings.net, Wed.–Sat. 10 A.M.–5 P.M., Sun. noon–5 P.M., tours $4), five miles south of downtown Knoxville. Sevier received 640 acres at the foot of Bays Mountain for his service in the Revolutionary War, and he named the property Marble Springs because there were marble deposits and a large spring. By 1792 Sevier established a farm residence at Marble Springs, although he and his family lived here only periodically. They also had a home in Knoxville.

After Sevier died in 1815, the property changed

hands several times until the State of Tennessee bought it in 1941. It remains state owned and is operated by the Gov. John Sevier Memorial Association. Over the years, the log home has been restored, and several historically accurate outbuildings have been added. Workshops and living-history days are offered year-round.

NORTH KNOXVILLE

Broadway (U.S. 441) travels from downtown Knoxville to Fountain City, an early suburb of the city.

Old Gray Cemetery

Just past Knoxville's scruffy Mission District—past the old 5th Avenue Hotel, a flophouse turned affordable housing project—is the Old Gray Cemetery (543 N. Broadway, 865/522-1424, www.oldgraycemetary.com). This 13-acre cemetery was established in 1850 and is the final resting place of hundreds of prominent and not-so-prominent city residents. It is a pleasant, wooded, parklike place—nice for a quiet stroll.

Among the buried are William "Parson" Brownlow, minister, journalist, governor, and one of Tennessee's most colorful historical characters; feminist Lizzie Crozier French; and C. C. Williams, the father of playwright Tennessee Williams.

Knoxville College

Presbyterian missionaries established a school for freedmen in Knoxville in 1875, and two years later this educational institution was designated as a college. Knoxville College (901 Knoxville College Dr., 865/524-6525) has been educating African Americans since. The campus is an architectural mixed bag—elegant historic structures share space with low-slung modern buildings. Budget challenges have dogged Knoxville College over its modern history, but it has persisted nonetheless in its mission to educate the next generation of black leaders.

Knoxville College is located in Mechanicsville, an old neighborhood found at the intersection of Western Avenue and Middlebrook Pike.

Entertainment and Events

Knoxville boasts a lively local music scene, plus venues that attract big-name artists. The arts scene also includes professional theater, dance, and music companies.

NIGHTLIFE

Downtown Knoxville offers plenty of options for entertainment after the sun sets.

The Old City

Near the intersection of Jackson and Depot Streets, a few blocks northeast of Gay Street, is the Old City. Knoxville's former warehouse district, near the train tracks, is now its chief entertainment district. Here you will find **Patrick Sullivan's** (100 N. Central St., 865/637-4255),

an Irish-inspired restaurant and bar that is a good place to meet for drinks.

Barley's Taproom and Pizzeria (200 E. Jackson St., 865/521-0092, cover varies) is a large taproom with lots of space for mingling and a stage where folk, rock, and country performers can be found just about every night of the week. The 1st-floor bar offers 40 different beers on tap, a full-service restaurant, and a stage. Upstairs are pool tables and dartboards. Outside is a patio where you can witness Knoxville's skyline as you meet and mingle.

Downtown

Downtown nightlife centers on Market Square. Here you can catch up with friends at

Preservation Pub (28 Market Sq., 865/524-2224, cover varies). In the shadow of its exposed-brick walls decorated with funky art, you just can't help but feel cool. Fabulous drink specials; a hip, youthful attitude; and a steady stream of local rock, folk, and country acts make Preservation Pub a popular destination. It is also a restaurant.

Located in the Fourth and Gill neighborhood, a few blocks north of downtown, is the cozy and intimate **Sassy Ann's House of Blues** (820 N. 4th Ave., 865/525-5839, cover varies). As the name suggests, Sassy Ann's specializes in the blues—visiting musicians, homegrown talent, and open-mic-style performers—but they also book rock and folk artists. Housed in a 100-plus-year-old town house with two bars and lots of intimate pockets for seating, Sassy Ann's is a bit like going to a grown-up house party, with live music to boot. Generally speaking, Sassy Ann's has DJ music on Sunday and Thursday nights, with bands on Wednesday, Friday, and Saturday.

The Valarium (1213 Western Ave., 865/522-2820, cover varies) is a 1,000-person standing-only entertainment venue located under the Western Avenue Viaduct, in a seeming wasteland of highway interchanges. Once a venue for cutting-edge bands, then a gay dance hall, this cavernous hall now books performing artists of all types. The bar is outside, allowing the owners to make this an all-ages club.

THE ARTS
Venues
Knoxville's historic theaters are something special. In 1928 the **Tennessee Theatre** (604 S. Gay St., 865/684-1200, www.tennesseetheatre.com) opened its doors on Gay Street. The theater operated nearly uninterrupted for 50 years as a movie house and concert hall. After being shuttered for a few years, the theater operated during the 1980s and 1990s, although the venue was showing its age. Thankfully, in

2001 plans were announced for a full-fledged restoration that would bring the Tennessee back to its former glory.

Since 2005, when the Tennessee Theatre reopened to praise from concertgoers and performers alike, it has become Knoxville's favorite venue for music, theater, and film. Its interior is awash with ornate detail, including plush fabric, intricate woodwork, gold-painted trim, and glistening chandeliers—all reminiscent of the roaring twenties, when the theater was built. The theater's 1928 original Mighty Wurlitzer pipe organ is also a showstopper.

Check the theater's website for upcoming performances for an opportunity to experience entertainment at its finest. You can also call to request a tour of the theater, if no show is in the offing.

Knoxville's best-sounding concert hall is also located on Gay Street. The **Bijou Theater** (803 S. Gay St., 865/522-0832, www.knoxbijou.com) opened in 1909 as part of the Lamar Hotel. Since then, it has been a venue for concerts and other performances. With a capacity of 700, it is more intimate than the Tennessee Theatre; it is also far less ornate and upscale. The Bijou underwent restoration in 2005, which resulted in a brand-new sound and stage system, better seats, and a new heating and air-conditioning system.

Other Knoxville concert and theater venues include the **Knoxville Civic Auditorium and Coliseum** (500 E. Church Ave., 865/215-8999, www.knoxvillecoliseum.com), which seats 2,500, and the **Thompson-Boling Arena** (1600 Phillip Fulmer Way, 865/974-0953, www.tbarena.com), with a capacity of almost 25,000.

Dance and Opera
The **Appalachian Ballet Company** (865/982-8463, www.appalachianballet.com) is a regional dance group chartered in 1972. The company puts on three performances each year, including a holiday production of *The Nutcracker*.

Circle Modern Dance (865/309-5309, www.

circlemoderndance.com) is a grassroots dance group founded in 1990 to provide an alternative to mainstream dance performances. They offer classes as well as the occasional show.

The **Knoxville Opera** (865/524-0795, www.knoxvilleopera.com) offers four performances annually at the Tennessee Theatre in downtown Knoxville. The opera also organizes the Rossini Festival and International Street Fair, an Italian street fair, every April.

Theater

The University of Tennessee's **Clarence Brown Theatre Company** (865/974-5161, www.clarencebrowntheatre.com) presents a wide repertoire of plays featuring nationally and internationally recognized guest artists. The company performs in the 570-seat Clarence Brown Theatre (1714 Andy Holt Blvd.) on the UT campus, named for UT alumnus and distinguished film director Clarence Brown. UT is also home to the 350-seat Ula Love Doughty Carousel Theater and a 100-seat black-box theater, which are used for campus productions.

Knoxville's **Carpetbag Theatre** (865/544-0447, www.carpetbagtheatre.org) is a community-based nonprofit professional theater company founded in 1970. It is one of the few tenured African American professional theater companies in the South. The company produces plays, festivals, youth theater workshops, and other events throughout the year. Their performances often bring to the fore the stories and experiences of people who are otherwise overlooked by history.

The **Tennessee Stage Company** (865/546-4280, www.tennesseestagecompany.com) produces Shakespeare in the Square, a free summertime production of Shakespeare's work at Market Square Mall, and the New Play Festival, which brings to life unpublished theatrical works.

Music
◖ WDVX BLUE PLATE SPECIAL
Back in the 1930s and '40s, Knoxville radio station WNOX hosted a lunchtime musical variety show called the *Midday Merry-Go-Round*. Hosted by Lowell Blanchard, the show attracted hundreds of patrons and thousands more who tuned in to listen to the show live on radio. It was a stepping stone to the Grand Ole Opry, and legendary performers like Roy Acuff, Chet Atkins, Kitty Wells, and Bill and Charlie Monroe were among the entertainers.

So when Knoxville radio station WDVX started its own lunchtime live music program back in the 1990s, it was following in hallowed footsteps. But it also felt like something quite new and exciting for downtown Knoxville.

Today, the WDVX Blue Plate Special takes place Monday–Friday noon–1 P.M. at the Knoxville Visitor Center at 301 South Gay Street (the building also houses the WDVX studios). The performers vary from bluegrass to Americana to rock. It is a wonderful way to pass an hour since you get to listen to live music and watch a radio show being made at the same time. The atmosphere is intimate, casual, and—at times—electric. A coffee bar serves sandwiches and drinks, but you are welcome to bring your own bag lunch as well.

KNOXVILLE SYMPHONY ORCHESTRA
Established in 1935, the Knoxville Symphony Orchestra (865/291-3310, www.knoxvillesymphony.com) is one of the oldest orchestras in the southeast. The KSO, a professional orchestra since 1973, performs its season September–May in Knoxville venues including the Civil Auditorium, the Tennessee Theatre, and the Bijou. Special guest conductors and soloists are frequent additions, and seasonal shows include the annual holiday concert.

UNIVERSITY OF TENNESSEE
The University of Tennessee's music program (www.music.utk.edu) puts on a full schedule of recitals and concerts during the academic year. All events are free and open to the public. They take place in one of three performance halls in the **Alumni Memorial Building** (1408 Middle Dr.).

JUBILEE COMMUNITY ARTS

One of Knoxville's finest musical institutions is Jubilee Community Arts, which promotes traditional Appalachian music and other folk traditions. Jubilee offers a full schedule of concerts and other special events at the **Laurel Theater** (1538 Laurel Ave., 865/522-5851, www.jubileearts.org), a 19th-century church in the Fort Sanders neighborhood that has been converted into a performance hall. The space is intimate, with excellent acoustics and a homey atmosphere. The concert schedule is heavy on regional bluegrass, folk, Americana, and country performers. It also includes Celtic, zydeco, and world music artists. Concerts are scheduled most weeks. The Jubilee Festival in March is a three-day weekend event with a smorgasbord of performances.

When the Laurel Theater is not being used for a concert, various community groups use the space for meetings and other purposes. Several community dance groups have weekly sessions here, as does the Knoxville Writer's Guild. In addition to its live performance schedule, Jubilee Community Arts works with local radio stations to produce programming for the airwaves, including the long-running *Live at Laurel* program, which features recordings of Laurel Theater concerts and is broadcast on WDVX (89.9 FM and 102.9 FM) at 7 P.M. on Sunday.

Cinemas

First-run movies came back to downtown Knoxville with the opening of **Regal Cinemas Riviera Stadium** (510 S. Gay St., 865/522-5160), an eight-screen theater in the heart of downtown.

Knoxville's best art-house movie theater is at **Downtown West** (1640 Downtown West Blvd., 865/693-6327), in the West Hills area near West Town Mall.

FESTIVALS AND EVENTS

Spring

Knoxville's stalwart arts festival celebrated its 50th anniversary in 2010. The **Dogwood Arts Festival** (www.dogwoodarts.com) takes place in April to coincide with the springtime blooming of dogwood trees. The core of the festival is the opening of 70 miles of dogwood trails that pass through historic and architecturally significant neighborhoods and by thousands of blooming dogwood trees.

The Dogwood Arts Festival also includes a variety of art shows and other events—workshops, festivals, and concerts—aimed at promoting the arts in the community and in area schools.

In April, the Knoxville Opera organizes the **Rossini Festival** (www.rossinifestival.org), an Italian street fair that takes place on Gay Street and at Market Square Mall in downtown Knoxville. Special wine tastings, opera performances, and European music combine with a vibrant street fair with a pronounced Mediterranean theme.

Summer

The **Kuumba Festival** is an African-inspired street festival that takes place in late June at Market Square downtown and in Chilhowee Park in East Knoxville. The event features parades, music, arts demonstrations, and vendors, all with an African theme.

The end of summer is marked annually with **Boomsday,** the largest fireworks display in the nation over the Tennessee River, on Labor Day.

Shopping

GAY STREET

Some of Knoxville's most distinctive stores are found on Gay Street. The first **Mast General Store** (402 S. Gay St., 865/546-1336, Mon.–Wed. 10 A.M.–6 P.M., Thurs.–Sat. 10 A.M.–9 P.M.) opened in Valle Crucis, North Carolina, in 1883, and it sold everything that folks needed, "from cradles to caskets," as it is said. Mast is now a chain with locations in several Southern mountain cities, including Asheville, North Carolina, and Greenville, South Carolina. Like the others, Knoxville's Mast General Store sells a satisfying variety of sturdy clothing and footwear, classic cookware like cast-iron skillets, old-fashioned candy, and games.

Also on Gay Street, the **East Tennessee Historical Society Gift Shop** (601 S. Gay St., 865/215-8824, Mon.–Sat. 10 A.M.–4 P.M., Sun. 1–5 P.M.) has a good collection of books about Tennessee, local arts and crafts, and T-shirts from the 1982 World's Fair.

GALLERIES

Gay Street is a major contributor to Knoxville's vibrant gallery scene. Knoxville's Arts & Culture Alliance manages an art gallery in an old furniture store at the **Emporium Center for Arts & Culture** (100 S. Gay St., 865/523-7543, www.theemporiumcenter.com, Mon.–Fri. 9 A.M.–5 P.M., free). Home to two art galleries, the Emporium puts on 12 different shows annually that showcase local and regional arts.

The Emporium also provides studio space for area artists and office space for arts organizations. The galleries are open until 9 P.M. on the first Friday of each month and 11 A.M.–3 P.M. on the first Saturday of each month.

Located next door to the Emporium galleries is a downtown satellite of UT's Ewing Gallery. The **University of Tennessee Downtown Gallery** (106 S. Gay St., 865/673-0802, Wed.–Fri. 11 A.M.–6 P.M., Sat. 10 A.M.–3 P.M., free) has a modern, fresh feel. Student and faculty artwork are exhibited alongside shows of regional and national artists.

The Art Market (422 S. Gay St., 865/525-5265, Mon.–Sat. 11 A.M.–6 P.M., Sun. 1–5 P.M.) is a stalwart artists' cooperative that traces its roots to the 1982 World's Fair. More than 60 area painters, sculptures, jewelers, weavers, and printmakers display their work at this attractive and welcoming space.

BOOKSTORES

Central Street Books (842 N. Central St., 865/573-9959, Mon.–Sat. 11 A.M.–6 P.M., Sun. 1 P.M.–5 P.M., call for winter hours) is an above-average used-book store with a notable collection of local books and collector's editions. As a bonus, it's located next to Magpie Bakery, reportedly the best bakery in Knoxville.

Another option for used books is **McKay's** (230 Papermill Place Way, 865/588-0331, Mon.–Thurs. 9 A.M.–9 P.M., Fri.–Sat. 9 A.M.–10 P.M., Sun. 11 A.M.–7 P.M.), a warehouse-size bookstore that is well organized and well loved by readers of all stripes. McKay's also has a giant location on the west side of Nashville.

The closest new-book store to downtown Knoxville is **Barnes and Noble** (8029 Kingston Pk., 865/670-0773, Mon.–Thurs. 9 A.M.–10 P.M., Fri.–Sat. 9 A.M.–11 P.M., Sun. 11 A.M.–9 P.M.), located next to West Town Mall.

KNOXVILLE

Sports and Recreation

Sports may be Knoxville's single biggest draw. The University of Tennessee Vols play football at Neyland Stadium, on the banks of the Tennessee River. The Lady Vols basketball team is the most successful sports team at UT. There are sporting events and sports museums and, of course, plenty of sports fans.

But Knoxville is more than just UT sports. There are nice parks, too.

PARKS

Knoxville has more than two dozen city parks. For a complete list of parks and facilities, visit the city website (www.cityofknoxville.org).

World's Fair Park

Knoxville's best city park is the 10-acre World's Fair Park, which connects downtown with UT and brings new life to the site of the 1982 World's Fair. The park consists of walking paths, fountains, a man-made lake, grassy spaces, and a statue of Russian musician and composer Sergei Rachmaninoff, whose last public performance was at UT on February 17, 1943. The fountains are a popular attraction on hot summer days, when families come to romp in the water.

North of the fountains and adjacent to the East Tennessee Veteran's Memorial is a 4,150-square-foot playground that features a climbing wall, neutron spinner, several slides, a dual-track ride, and more. Features included were chosen by local elementary school students for their fun factor.

Tyson Park

Located at the western edge of the UT campus along Alcoa Highway, Tyson Park is a venerable city park with playgrounds, picnic tables, walking paths, tennis courts, and a skate park.

Sequoyah Park

Located in West Knoxville on the banks of the Tennessee River, 87-acre Sequoyah Park is a good place for walking, biking, or relaxing outdoors. There are playgrounds, baseball/softball fields, and lots of open space ideal for a picnic or game of Frisbee.

Sequoyah is located at 1400 Cherokee Boulevard. Get there by driving west on Kingston Pike and turning left onto Cherokee Boulevard.

Chilhowee Park

Chilhowee Park (3301 Magnolia Ave.), located off Magnolia Avenue in East Knoxville, was the city's first major park. The first streetcar line in the city connected downtown with Chilhowee, and on weekends, holidays, and hot summer days, throngs would come here to picnic, splash in the lake, or watch baseball games, horse races, or concerts.

Today the reasons to head here are spectator driven rather than recreational, such as tractor pulls and gun expos. The Knoxville Zoo, Knox County Fairgrounds, and East Tennessee Science Discovery Center all abut Chilhowee Park for a nearby recreation bonanza.

Greenways

Knoxville has an expanding array of greenways that connect parks and make it possible to get around the city on foot or by bike. Those of special note include the **James White Greenway** that originates at the South Knoxville bridge and follows the Tennessee River to Volunteer Landing downtown. On the other end of Volunteer Landing, you can follow the **Neyland Greenway** to Tyson Park and onward to the **Third Creek Greenway,** which connects with both the **Bearden Greenway** and the **Sequoyah Greenway.**

On the south side of the river, the **Will Skelton Greenway** begins at Island Home Park, passes through Ijams Nature Center, and follows the shore of the Tennessee to the Forks of the River.

For information about Knoxville greenways, go to www.cityofknoxville.org/greenways or call 865/215-4311 for the Parks and Recreation Department. The Knox Greenways Coalition (865/215-2807, www.knoxgreenwayscoalition.com) supports the use and development of greenways in the city.

Knoxville Botanical Garden and Arboretum

The Knoxville Botanical Garden and Arboretum (2743 Wimpole St., 865/862-8717, www.knoxarboretum.org, daily sunrise–sunset, free) is a dream that is slowly taking shape. Located on grounds once occupied by a plant nursery, the gardens are an effort by volunteers and family members of the former landowners.

The grounds are leafy and pleasant, though not very manicured. It is a pleasant place to come for a walk. Staff members are generally present on weekdays 9 A.M.–5 P.M.; at other times the garden is unattended.

SPECATATOR SPORTS

Watching sports in Knoxville means one thing: the University of Tennessee Volunteers. Knoxville is the epicenter of Big Orange country, and this is a city that is serious about sports. UT is a member of the competitive Southeastern Conference.

Football

UT's biggest spectator sport is football. Neyland Stadium, home of the football team, is awash with bright orange on game days. Named for Gen. Robert Neyland, head coach of the UT football team from 1926 to 1952, Neyland Stadium has a capacity of just over 100,000. Most home games sell out.

The regular college football season runs September–November. Single tickets go on sale in late July or early August for the upcoming fall season and cost $45–90. You can buy tickets from the **UT box office** (1600 Phillip Fulmer

Way, 865/656-1200, www.utsports.com). On game days, tickets are sold at Gate 21 at Neyland Stadium beginning four hours before kickoff.

A word to the wise: If you are not coming into town to watch the football game, avoid downtown Knoxville on a game day. The entire city becomes a knot of congestion and Big Orange mania on these days, and if you don't want to be part of it, you'll hate the experience. Longtime residents who don't particularly fancy college football say that game days are good times to go to the mall, visit the Great Smoky Mountains National Park, or just stay home. Whatever you do, plan ahead.

Basketball

In Knoxville, UT's men's basketball team plays second fiddle to the legendary Lady Vols, eight-time national champions who have been leaders of the women's college basketball pack for a generation. The Lady Vols, under the leadership of coach Holly Warlick, play home games at Thompson-Boling Arena November–March.

Single-game tickets go on sale in October and cost $45–80 depending on your seat and the opponent. Buy tickets from the **UT box office** (1600 Phillip Fulmer Way, 865/565-1200, www.utladyvols.com).

Other UT Sports

UT plays a full schedule of sports: track and field, baseball, softball, tennis, soccer, rowing, tennis, swimming, golf, and volleyball. The UT women's softball team has performed well in recent years and is developing a reputation as a Southeastern Conference leader. UT tennis and track have good records, and in 2010 the university built a new golf center to bolster its program in that sport. For a full rundown of UT sports events, contact the athletics box office (1600 Phillip Fulmer Way, 865/656-1200, www.utsports.com).

Ice Hockey

The **Knoxville Ice Bears** (www.knoxvilleicebears.com) play at the Knoxville Civic Coliseum. The Ice

Bears are a member of the Southern Professional Hockey League and play October–April.

TOURS

The **Three Rivers Rambler** (Volunteer Landing, 865/524-9411, www.threeriversrambler.com, adults $26.50, seniors $25.50, children 3–12 $15.50, toddlers 1–2 $7.50) is an 11-mile scenic railroad excursion that departs from downtown Knoxville. The ride travels along the Tennessee River past Island Home airport to the confluence of the Holston and French Broad Rivers. The journey takes 90 minutes and takes you past farmland and old quarries. The open-air car is a real treat in pleasant weather.

Rambles take place on holiday weekends such as Father's Day, Independence Day, and Halloween. Call ahead for a current schedule. You can reserve tickets online or up to 30 minutes before departure at the ticket counter.

To get to the Three Rivers Rambler, take Neyland Drive (Highway 158) along the Tennessee River. Look for parking lot C-18 on the shore side of the road, where Rambler guests may park for free.

The **Tennessee Riverboat Company** (300 Neyland Dr., 865/525-7827, www.tnriverboat.com) offers dinner cruises and daytime sightseeing cruises down the Tennessee River on an old-fashioned paddleboat.

Accommodations

On the up side, Knoxville's downtown hotel rooms run a bit cheaper than those in other major Tennessee cities. On the down side, the city has one of the highest combined sales- and room-tax rates in the state: 17.25 percent. Be sure to figure this in when planning your budget.

DOWNTOWN

There is a pleasant array of boutique and chain hotels in downtown Knoxville, many of which are convenient to Gay Street, Market Square, and the riverfront.

$100-150

Knoxville's most distinctive hotel is a bit hard to find. The renovated and renamed **❰ Oliver Hotel** (407 Union Ave., 865/521-0050, www.theoliverhotel.com, $135–278) is located just around the corner from Market Square, but the 1876 town house easily blends into its surroundings. Built by German baker Peter Kern in the 19th century, the former St. Oliver was converted into a hotel for the 1982 World's Fair. It is not well advertised, but patrons find

it nonetheless. Far from the cookie-cutter, the Oliver Hotel offers superior location and genuinely friendly service. Its 24 guest rooms have elegant beds, refrigerators, wet bars, and coffee service. Perhaps the best perk is the downstairs library, with soft couches and inviting reading nooks that beg you to come in and sit a spell.

Offering an ideal location and intimate, personalized service, the **❰ Maplehurst Inn** (800 W. Hill Ave., 865/254-5240, www.maplehurstinn.com, $79–145) is worth considering. Each of the 11 guest rooms has a private bath and personalized touches to make you feel like you're at home. Breakfast is served in a cozy dining room overlooking the Tennessee River. Maplehurst dates from the early 20th century, when the town house was built for a wealthy merchant. It was converted to a bed-and-breakfast for the 1982 World's Fair and remains one of the only bed-and-breakfasts in downtown Knoxville.

Located at the north end of downtown, near the Old City and Gay Street, is the **Crowne Plaza Knoxville** (401 W. Summit Hill Dr., 865/522-2600, $144–174). This 197-room

©ETHAN ORLEY

The renovated Oliver Hotel is now a landmark and a Market Square must-stay.

The **Hilton Knoxville** (501 W. Church Ave., 865/523-2300, $99–159) is a high-rise hotel located in the midst of downtown office buildings. It is a few blocks from Gay Street and Market Square Mall. The Hilton offers guest rooms, suites, and executive guest rooms with upgraded amenities and the best views of the city. There is a business center, fitness room, pool, cribs and high chairs for children, an on-site ATM, car rental, and café.

Over $200

Feel like part of Knoxville's downtown renaissance at **Cook Loft** (722 S. Gay St., 865/310-2216, www.cookloft.com, $450–500), an urban guesthouse and event venue. Skylights, hardwood floors, high ceilings, exposed-brick walls, large windows, and sleek lines bring the loft concept to life. Two bedrooms and a spacious living room invite you to relax and spread out. The kitchen is well furnished with restaurant-grade appliances, but you probably won't be doing much cooking with all the great restaurants in your backyard. Weekly rates ($2,100) are also available.

high-rise hotel has full business services, an indoor pool and fitness center, 24-hour lounge, and updated guest rooms.

$150-200

Located in a pyramid-shaped building on the Knoxville waterfront, the **Knoxville Marriott** (500 Hill Ave. SE, 865/637-1234, $119–169) is one of the city's most distinctive landmarks. The unusual design creates a lofty lobby and gives many of the guest rooms impressive river views. In addition to novelty, the Marriott also offers its guests a slew of thoughtful amenities especially designed for business travelers. There is an outdoor swimming pool, fitness center, and full-service salon on-site. There are also two restaurants, a gift shop, and lots of meeting space. The Knoxville Marriott is located next door to the Women's Basketball Hall of Fame and is within walking distance of downtown attractions like Blount Mansion and James White Fort.

UNIVERSITY OF TENNESSEE
$100-150

Located near the World's Fair Park on the edge of Fort Sanders, the **Cumberland House Hotel** (1109 White Ave., 865/971-4663, $145–175) is a Sheraton. The 130 guest rooms have flat-screen televisions, coffeemakers, hair dryers, and CD players. Suites with kitchenettes and couches are available. The hotel, built in 2005, boasts an on-site restaurant as well as a fitness center. Cumberland House is convenient to UT and to Neyland Stadium.

FOURTH AND GILL
Under $100

The historic residential neighborhood of Fourth and Gill, near the Old City and slightly north of downtown, is home to the **Knoxville**

KNOXVILLE

Hostel (404 Fourth Ave., 865/546-8090, $17). Located in a homey urban cottage with hardwood floors, a generous porch, and small backyard, the Knoxville Hostel offers its guests bunk-bed dorm-style accommodation in sex-segregated bedrooms. Guests can lounge by the TV, use the kitchen, or surf the Internet for free on the hostel computer. Linens are provided, as is a free continental breakfast. All in all, it's a good deal, even for the budget conscious. The hostel is within walking distance of the Old City, Gay Street, and the trolley line.

WEST KNOXVILLE
$100-150

There's no shortage of chain hotels and chain restaurants in the development near Turkey Creek Medical Center. But that means you get reliably clean, safe, albeit not necessarily interesting, places to sleep. Top among them is the **Homewood Suites** (10935 Turkey Dr., 865/777-0375, $99–139). A friendly staff, easy parking, and free access to a nearby gym make it an easy place to stay.

Food

Knoxville dining is impossible to pigeonhole. Downtown eateries cater to the business lunch crowd, college students, and downtown's new young professional residents. Older neighborhoods outside of the city center are home to hole-in-the-wall eateries that defy expectation.

Whatever you do, don't head straight for the familiar chain restaurant. Explore a bit; you'll be richly rewarded.

DOWNTOWN

Gay Street, the Old City, and Market Square have a large concentration of restaurants that cater to all tastes and budgets.

Casual

For coffee, baked treats, and sandwiches, grab a table at **Old City Java** (109 S. Central St., 865/523-9817, Mon.–Fri. 7 A.M.–10 P.M., Sat.–Sun. 8 A.M.–10 P.M., $4–9). Hardwood floors, plenty of cozy tables, and wireless Internet make this a popular place to while away a few hours.

Market Square's most celebrated restaurant is ◖ **The Tomato Head** (12 Market Sq., 865/637-4067, Mon. 11 A.M.–3 P.M., Tues.–Thurs. 11 A.M.–10 P.M., Fri. 11 A.M.–11 P.M., Sat. 10 A.M.–11 P.M., Sun. 10 A.M.–9 P.M., $4–9), which opened its doors downtown long before

it was cool. Originally a pizza joint, the Tomato Head now serves soup, sandwiches, salads, burritos, and pizza made with only the best organic and otherwise pure-at-heart ingredients. The results are way above average. Vegetarians and meat eaters can rejoice, for options range from a vegetarian sandwich made with flavorful tofu to a roast beef sandwich heaped with meat. The pizza is still mighty popular, and for good reason. They offer 14 official varieties, but you can build your own pie from a list of 45 different toppings (homemade lamb sausage, anyone?). The Tomato Head is generally crowded and noisy. You step to the counter, order, and pay, and then one of the low-key staff members will bring your order to the table. It's a good meeting place and also a great place for a quick solo lunch. The owners are working on another location in West Knoxville (the one in downtown Maryville closed). They also own Flour Head bakery.

The **Downtown Grill & Brewery** (424 S. Gay St., 865/633-8111, Sun.–Thurs. 11 A.M.–midnight, Fri.–Sat. 11 A.M.–3 A.M., $8–18) is as popular for its selection of handcrafted brews as it is for its easy bar-style menu. Mesquite-grilled steak, jumbo pasta plates, pizza, and fajitas all come with a recommendation from the chef for the right beer accompaniment. With outdoor sidewalk seating and a prime location on Gay Street, this is a popular restaurant to meet and mingle.

Pete's Coffee Shop (540 Union Ave., 865/523-2860, Mon.–Fri. 6:30 A.M.–2:30 P.M., Sat. 7 A.M.–2 P.M., $4–10) is the best downtown destination for diner-style breakfasts and plate lunches. Located in a storefront a few blocks from Market Square, Pete's attracts a loyal following among downtown office workers and new residents. It is the type of place that offers you a bottomless cup of joe and no-nonsense food like club sandwiches, fried chicken, and omelets.

Japanese

Handcrafted sushi along with cuisine that fuses Japanese, Korean, and Spanish ingredients and styles: That is what **Nama** (506 S. Gay St., 865/633-8539, Mon.–Sat. 11 A.M.–midnight, Sun. noon–midnight, $8–25), a trendy sushi house on Gay Street, offers. The enlightened business set dines here at lunchtime; at night it attracts a youthful, well-heeled crowd. The half-price maki happy hour 4–6 P.M. is a good deal for the budget diner.

Fusion

C 31 Bistro (31 Market Sq., 865/566-0275, Mon.–Fri. 11 A.M.–3 P.M. and 4 P.M.–midnight, Sat. 10 A.M.–3 P.M. and 4 P.M.–midnight, Sun. 10 A.M.–3 P.M., $16–23) offers a serious farm-to-table commitment in a cozy Market Square storefront. The seasonally changing menu offers Southern-fusion shrimp and grits, mountain trout with sage butter, and select local cuts of beef. Brunch is served on weekends.

English

Who knew that English cuisine would have its day? **C The Crown & Goose** (123 S. Central St., 865/524-2100, Mon.–Thurs. 11 A.M.–11 P.M., Fri. 11 A.M.–2 A.M., Sat. noon–2 A.M., Sun. 11 A.M.–4 P.M., $12–28) in the Old City is proving that Welsh rarebit, fish-and-chips, and bangers and mash are indeed good food. But to be fair, the Crown & Goose is far more than British Isle pub food. They have adopted the best of the Continent, as well, and put it on display in dishes like spring vegetable and wild mushroom risotto, San Marzano tomato and Stilton bisque, and the Frenchman's Lunch, a European cheese board served with bread. Best of all, the Crown & Goose has a stylish but unpretentious atmosphere. This is a nice choice for an unexpectedly good dinner.

Sandwiches

Hefty sandwiches on home-baked bread keep the patrons coming to venerable **Steamboat Sandwiches** (7 Market Sq., 865/546-3333, Mon.–Fri. 10 A.M.–8 P.M., Sat. 11 A.M.–8 P.M., Sun. 11 A.M.–3 P.M., $5–8). The Steamboat is an oversized sandwich packed with ham, Genoa salami, and swiss cheese, finished with a mild hot sauce, mayonnaise, mustard, and pickle. Thankfully for those with smaller appetites, you can also order a half size.

UNIVERSITY OF TENNESSEE
Fusion

Knoxville's best restaurant for vegetarians is the **Sunspot** (1909 Cumberland Ave., 865/637-4663, Mon.–Sat. 11 A.M.–10 P.M., Sun. 10:30 A.M.–10 P.M., limited late-night menu, $8–17), an institution on the UT strip that features eclectic cuisine with strong Southwestern and Latin American influences. For vegetarians there is the baked enchilada, the Tofu Tier (a stack of baked tofu and fried eggplant in a savory miso sauce), and an awesome veggie burger. Carnivores have options like pan-seared tilapia served over cheese grits, and Pasta Rustica, chorizo sausage and red peppers served in a spicy tomato sauce. There are dozens of beers on tap and in the bottle.

WEST KNOXVILLE
Fine Dining

For a taste of Knoxville's most elegant food,

make reservations at **The Orangery** (5412 Kingston Pk., 865/588-2964, Mon.–Thurs. 11:30 A.M.–2 P.M. and 5:30–10 P.M., Fri. 11:30 A.M.–2 P.M. and 5:30–11 P.M., Sat. 5:30–11 P.M., lunch $9–14, dinner $23–44). A French-inspired menu, impeccable wine list, and refined atmosphere make for a luxurious dining experience. Come for lunch for salad Niçoise, roasted-vegetable ravioli, and sautéed shrimp. Dinner specialties include veal porterhouse, prime New York strip, buffalo with caramelized shallots, and elk chop with vegetable puree. Bet you can't get that at home. Also consider the $35 prix fixe menu, which begins with an amuse-bouche and ends four courses later with desserts such as raspberry tiramisu or an amaretto brownie served with whipped cream and caramel pecan sauce.

Italian
The best New York–style pizzas, handcrafted calzones, and other authentic Italian favorites are offered at **Savelli's** (3055 Sutherland Ave., 865/521-9085, Mon.–Thurs. 11 A.M.–9 P.M., Fri.–Sat. 11 A.M.–10 P.M., $9–19). This homey restaurant is small and often crowded, for good reason: Savelli's serves made-from-scratch Italian food at good prices. Beer is served, but bring your own wine.

SOUTH KNOXVILLE
Steak
Beef lovers rule at **Ye Olde Steak House** (6838 Chapman Hwy., 865/577-9328, Sun.–Thurs. 4–9 P.M., Fri.–Sat. 4–9:30 P.M., $12–35), where the menu features nearly a dozen different cuts of beef, including a generous hand-patted burger. Seafood and chicken are also served. Ye Olde Steak House is a family-owned steak house set in a Tudor-style home (hence the name). It is a funky, family-friendly destination for diners with big appetites.

Beer is served at Ye Olde Steak House, but liquor and wine are not. You may bring your own.

Middle Eastern
For a dining experience like no other, head directly to ◖ **King Tut Grill** (4132 Martin Mill Pk., 865/573-6021, daily 11 A.M.–8 P.M., $6–12), a family-owned restaurant in otherwise unremarkable Vestal, a few miles south of the Henley Street bridge. King Tut's has established a loyal following thanks largely to the charisma of its owner, Mo, who serves drinks in flower vases, tells you what to order, and is famous for sending out extra food to his favored customers. Mo and his family offer traditional diner-style meals—hamburgers, meat loaf, baked chicken, and the like—to appease the locals, but the reason to come here is to eat home-style Egyptian fare. The daily menu offers a handful of such favorites, like falafel sandwiches, an Egyptian platter, and the best Greek salad in Knoxville. But it is on Mo's Middle Eastern night that he and his family go all out with stuffed grape leaves, homemade *basboosa,* and the works. Believe what they tell you: This is a restaurant not to be missed.

EAST KNOXVILLE
Southern
Arguably Knoxville's best meat-and-three Southern-food house, **Chandlers** (3101 E. Magnolia Ave., 865/595-0212, Mon. 11 A.M.–3 P.M., Tues.–Thurs. 11 A.M.–7:30 P.M., Fri. 11 A.M.–8:30 P.M., Sat. noon–8:30 P.M., Sun. noon–6 P.M., $4–10) is a cafeteria-style restaurant where workingmen and businesspeople rub elbows when the dinner bell rings. The fried chicken is always reliable and comes with sides like hot rolls, collard greens, fried okra, and stewed apples.

NORTH KNOXVILLE
Diners
◖ **Litton's** (2803 Essary Dr., 865/688-0429, Mon.–Thurs. 11 A.M.–8 P.M., Fri.–Sat. 11 A.M.–9:30 P.M., $7–17) is a North Knoxville institution where Knoxvillians go for the city's best

burgers, blue-plate lunches, and homemade dessert. Hand-cut fries, jumbo onion rings, red velvet cake, and baked sweet potatoes are some of the things that keep people coming back to Litton's again and again. A family restaurant that began as a humble grocery in 1946, Litton's is worth the drive. To get there, drive north on Broadway (U.S. 441), passing the I-640 overpass. Litton's is located across the street from the Fountain City park.

Information and Services

VISITOR INFORMATION

For information about Knoxville, contact the **Knoxville Tourism & Sports Corporation** (865/523-7263 or 800/727-8045, www.knoxville.org).

Downtown Knoxville (17 Market Sq., 865/637-4550, www.downtownknoxville.org) promotes the city center by publishing maps and guides, and maintaining a website.

The **Knoxville Visitor Center** (301 S. Gay St., 865/523-7263, Mon.–Fri. 8:30 A.M.–5 P.M., Sat. 9 A.M.–5 P.M., Sun. noon–4 P.M.) is at the corner of Gay Street and Summit Hill Drive. This is the place to pick up information and maps, but it is also a Knoxville gift shop and bookstore, wireless Internet hot spot, and the venue of the weekday WDVX Blue Plate Special, a midday concert and live radio broadcast. The coffee bar serves hot beverages, basic sandwiches, and sweets.

NEWSPAPERS

Knoxville's daily paper is the *Knoxville News Sentinel* (www.knoxnews.com). Its alternative weekly, *Metropulse* (www.metropulse.com), is a far better read. Smart commentary, up-to-date entertainment listings, and columns like "Secret History" make it great. Pick yours up free on Wednesday at local groceries, coffee shops, and restaurants.

RADIO

The Knoxville radio dial is crowded with the usual suspects, but a few frequencies are worth seeking out. Chief among them is **WDVX** (89.9 FM and 102.9 FM), a community-supported grassroots radio station that plays a mix of early country, contemporary Americana, and other roots music.

WUOT (91.9 FM) is the university's public radio station. It airs NPR news programs and classical music.

LIBRARIES

Knoxville's main public library is the **Lawson McGhee Library** (500 W. Church Ave., 865/215-8750, Mon.–Thurs. 9 A.M.–8 P.M., Fri. 9 A.M.–5:30 P.M., Sat. 10 A.M.–5 P.M., Sun. 1–5 P.M.). It has public Internet access.

GAY AND LESBIAN RESOURCES

In 2012, standard-bearer *The Advocate* named Knoxville the eighth most gay-friendly city in the United States, citing the university's LGBT groups, the Tennessee Valley Unitarian Universalist Church (www.tvuuc.org), and the gay softball league as some of the evidence of the welcoming community.

One place to network with LGBT people is at the **Metropolitan Community Church** (7820 Redeemer Ln., 865/531-2539, www.mccknoxville.org) in West Knoxville.

Getting There and Around

GETTING THERE
By Air

The **McGhee Tyson Airport** (TYS, www.tys. org) is the Knoxville area's airport. It is located 12 miles south of the city in Blount County.

A half dozen airlines serve McGhee Tyson with direct flights from 20 U.S. cities, including Orlando, Dallas, Houston, Denver, Memphis, Chicago, Cleveland, St. Paul, New York, Philadelphia, and Washington DC. Airlines with service to Knoxville include US Airways, United, Delta, American, Continental, Northwest, and Allegiant Air.

Taxis and car rentals are available at the airport. To get to downtown Knoxville from McGhee Tyson, take Alcoa Highway (U.S. 129) north to the city.

By Car

Two major interstate highways cross in Knoxville. I-75 is a north–south highway that connects with Lexington, Kentucky, in the north and Chattanooga to the south. I-40 is an east–west thoroughfare. About 35 miles east of Knoxville I-40 peels off and heads into North Carolina, while I-81 heads to the Tri-Cities and points northeast. I-40 west heads to Nashville and Memphis.

By Bus

Greyhound (www.greyhound.com) serves Knoxville with bus service to Nashville, Chattanooga, Asheville, Atlanta, and many other cities. The **Greyhound station** (100 East Magnolia Ave., 865/524-0369) is on Magnolia Avenue.

GETTING AROUND
Driving

Knoxville is a city where everyone drives to get where they're going. Sprawling suburbs, shopping malls, and the interstate are evidence of this.

I-640 is a bypass interstate that makes a circle on the northern fringe of Knoxville and allows I-40 through traffic to avoid downtown. Part of I-640 is also I-275.

While the interstate is efficient, there are good reasons to get off the highway. Thoroughfares like Cumberland/Kingston Pike, Chapman Highway/Henley Street/Broadway, and Central, Magnolia, and Western Avenues will give you a better sense of the character and geography of Knoxville. And with the possible exception of Kingston Pike, there's likely to be less traffic, too.

PARKING

Drive around downtown searching for a meter, or park in one of the many paid parking lots downtown. No matter what you do, all-day parking in Knoxville will rarely cost you more than $5 per day.

Public Transportation

The **Knoxville Trolley Line** (865/637-3000, www.katbus.com) offers free air-conditioned easy transit throughout downtown Knoxville most weekdays. The Vol Line (Mon.–Thurs 7 A.M.–6 P.M., Fri. 7 A.M.–10 P.M., Sat. 9 A.M.–10 P.M.) connects UT and the World's Fair Park with downtown, including Gay Street. The Downtown Loop (Mon.–Fri. 6 A.M.–6 P.M.) connects Hall of Fame Drive and the Civic Coliseum with Henley Street and downtown. The Gay Line runs on Gay Street to Hill (Mon.–Thurs 7 A.M.–6 P.M., Fri. 7 A.M.–10 P.M., Sat. 9 A.M.–10 P.M.).

Most Knoxville Trolleys are red, although sometimes orange Knoxville Transit Authority vans fill in. They stop at locations designated by a trolley sign.

Around Knoxville

CLINTON
◖ Green McAdoo Cultural Center

In 1955, Green McAdoo School was the segregated primary school for Clinton, a mill town of 4,000 people located about 20 miles northwest of Knoxville. Under the "separate but equal" policy of the segregationist South, graduates of the black primary school were bussed to Knoxville's all-black Austin High School for their secondary education.

Fifty years later, the school building became the Green McAdoo Cultural Center (101 School St., 865/463-6500, www.greenmcadoo. org, Tues.–Sat. 10 A.M.–5 P.M., free), which records and celebrates the remarkable story of the integration of Clinton's high school back in 1956. Don't speed, or you'll miss it—and this is definitely something you do not want to miss.

Tales of school desegregation in the South normally begin with Little Rock, Arkansas. But they really ought to begin with Clinton. That's because even before the Little Rock Six entered Little Rock Central High School in the fall of 1958, there were black and white students attending Clinton High School together in rural Tennessee.

In 1951, five black high school students petitioned the Anderson County Board of Education for the right to attend all-white Clinton High School. At this time, black students in Clinton were bussed a long 18 miles into Knoxville to attend the all-black Austin High School.

At first, the students lost their suit. U.S. District Judge Robert Taylor declared that the bussing arrangement met the requirements of separate but equal. However, when the U.S. Supreme Court decided the landmark Brown vs. Board of Education in the spring of 1954, Judge Taylor reversed his earlier ruling and ordered that Clinton High School be integrated at the beginning of the school term in September. What followed is a remarkable story,

recounted at the cultural center through newspaper clippings, video remembrances by the participants, and evocative photographs of the events. Integration went smoothly at first, but as the eyes of the world focused on this trendsetting Tennessee town, tensions began to run high. The National Guard was called in, and the school building was bombed. But the school principal, student body president, local Baptist minister, and other leaders in Clinton took a strong stand in favor of the rule of law—and, therefore, for integration.

One of the most moving displays in the museum is a glass case with letters that were received by Rev. Paul Turner, the white Baptist minister who helped to escort the black students to school and preached against the segregationists. There are anonymous and hateful postcards and letters that decry Rev. Turner, as well as letters of support from unknowns to celebrities, including Rev. Billy Graham and Edward R. Murrow.

Eventually, the world stopped paying a lot of attention to Clinton. New civil rights struggles were taking place all over the South, and the outsider segregationists who fomented the worst of the violence and unrest were gone. Photographers traveled to Clinton to take pictures when Bobby Cain became the first black male to graduate from a desegregated public school in May of 1957, but when Gail Epps followed in his footsteps the following year, no one paid any attention.

The events that took place in Clinton were recounted in an hour-long 1957 *See It Now* television program, and its 1960 sequel from CBS Reports, both of which may be seen at the museum. In 2006, the Green McAdoo Cultural Center produced an award-winning documentary about the events titled *Clinton 12,* which was narrated by James Earl Jones.

GRAINGER COUNTY AGRITOURISM

Grainger County lies northeast of Knoxville. One of the state's most rural counties, Grainger has a rugged landscape, defined by steep ridges and long valleys. The area is perhaps best known for its tomatoes–during the summer it is not uncommon to see farm stands set up around Knoxville with signs touting Grainger County Tomatoes.

You can get to the source of the abundance by visiting farms in Grainger County yourself. **Ritter Farms** (2999 Hwy. 11-W S., 865/767-2575, www.ritterfarms.com) is one of the largest family-owned farms in the area. They have a commercial kitchen where they prepare jams, jellies, salsas, and other farm-fresh provisions for retail sale. The farm market is open Monday-Saturday year-round; in the spring, summer, and fall you can buy seasonal fresh produce, and in winter they specialize in handicrafts, preserves, and baked goods. Call ahead to confirm hours. The farm is located between Bean Station and Rutledge.

Tennessee Homegrown Tomatoes (865/828-8316), located near Cherokee Lake on Route 375, about 3.5 miles east of Highway 92, grows all sorts of vegetables–not just tomatoes. They offer farm tours and host events throughout the growing season.

If you want some wine with your vegetables, you can get some at **Clinch Mountain Winery** (Thorn Hill, 865/767-3600, www.clinchmountainwinery.com, Mon.-Sat. 10 A.M.-7 P.M., Sun. noon-7 P.M.), located on Bullen Valley Road in the Thorn Hill community. Try their most popular varieties, Scooter Trash and Hound Dog Red, at the tasting room.

The crowning event for Grainger County farmers is the **Grainger County Tomato Festival** (www.graingercountytomatofestival.com), which takes place in Rutledge in late July every year.

Outside the museum is a life-size statue of the Clinton 12, the 12 African American young people who enrolled at Clinton High School in the fall of 1956. When the museum was opened in 2006, 9 of the 12 were on hand to see the statue being unveiled.

The Green McAdoo Cultural Center was funded in part by federal, state, and local funds, as well as through private donations. In 2007, legislation was introduced in Congress that would designate the Green McAdoo Cultural Center as part of the National Park Service.

The old Clinton High School building now houses Clinton Middle School, just a few blocks from the Green McAdoo center.

Get to Clinton by taking Clinton Highway (Highway 25 West) about 15 miles out of Knoxville. Once in Clinton, there are signs directing you to the center.

Appalachian Arts Craft Center

Locals love the Appalachian Arts Craft Center (2716 Andersonville Hwy., Norris, 865/494-9854, www.appalachianarts.net, Mon.–Sat. 10 A.M.–6 P.M., Sun. 1–5 P.M., closed Sun.–Mon. Jan.–Feb.) because they get to meet artists and learn to make works of art in ongoing workshops. But this small nonprofit gallery is a must-see for visitors, too, particularly if you want that one-of-kind souvenir to take home. Specialties include pottery, weaving, and quilting.

Museum of Appalachia

There is one place that every visitor to this region should visit if they are the least bit interested in the lifestyles and folk traditions of Appalachia. The Museum of Appalachia (2819 Andersonville Hwy., 865/494-7680, www.museumofappalachia.org, Jan.–Feb. daily 10 A.M.–5 P.M., Mar. and Nov.–Dec. daily 9 A.M.–5 P.M., Apr. weekdays 9 A.M.–5 P.M., weekends 9 A.M.–6 P.M., May–Oct. daily 9 A.M.–6 P.M. adults $18, seniors $15, teens 13–18 $10, children 5–12 $6) is one of a kind.

© BRIAN STANSBERRY/CREATIVE COMMONS

blacksmith shop at the Museum of Appalachia

Its 65 acres contain more of the history of this region than any other place in Tennessee. The collection includes more than 250,000 artifacts, and more than 100,000 people visit annually. This is all the more remarkable given that the museum, which is now a Smithsonian Institution affiliate, started as a collection from one man's garage.

The museum is a story told in several chapters. Its indoor exhibits include the Appalachian Hall of Fame, a remarkable collection of things that were made, used, and treasured by the people who came and created a life in the rugged land of the southern Appalachians. There are dolls that were whittled by rugged mountain men, banjos created from food tins, and the remains of a supposed perpetual motion machine. The exhibits are the work of John Rice Irwin, as is the whole museum. Irwin, a mountain man himself, has spent his life motivated by his admiration and love for the people who settled the mountains. He believes that the items of

everyday life are important, and that through them, we can understand the people who made them and made the region what it is. It certainly seems like he's right. Take the time to read the detailed and loving descriptions of each item in the hall of fame (most handwritten), and soon you will feel admiration and marvel for the people who made them, in the midst of what we would now consider hard times.

Music fans should not overlook the museum. Its collection of handmade fiddles, guitars, banjos, and mouth harps is unrivaled, and its displays about musicians tell not only who, what, and when, but also why and how. It's not to be missed.

Outside the hall of fame, the museum has a collection of mountain buildings. There is a log church, schoolhouse, pioneer homestead, and the log home where Mark Twain's parents lived in Possum Trot, Tennessee. As you explore these old buildings—all of which have been carefully moved from original locations throughout the region—look for members of the museum's menagerie: peacocks, horses, fainting goats, and sheep.

The Museum of Appalachia hosts several events during the year, but none is better known and as well loved than its annual **Homecoming** in October. The best musicians, writers, and artists come for the weekend, which offers the most authentic celebration of mountain arts in the region. Perhaps better loved by locals is the Fourth of July Anvil Shoot (yes, an actual anvil is shot into the air), which also includes music and crafts of the region.

In 2008, Irwin announced that he could no longer afford to keep the museum afloat with regular, large personal contributions, and locals, museumgoers, and historians alike were concerned that the museum would have to cut hours or otherwise look for cost-cutting measures. But his daughter, Elaine Irwin Meyer, took the reigns, forged the relationship with the Smithsonian, and took steps to preserve her father's legacy, and that of his forefathers, for the future.

Wear comfortable shoes, charge the camera battery, and prepare to stay for a good part of the day to see everything this site has to offer. Don't skip the gift shop or the on-site restaurant.

NORRIS DAM STATE PARK

TVA's first hydroelectric project was to construct a dam on the Clinch River, in Anderson County north of Knoxville. Construction of the 1,860-foot-long, 265-foot-tall dam started in 1933 and was completed in 1936. It was named for senator George Norris of Nebraska, who conceived of and championed the idea of a public power company in the Tennessee Valley. This was one of a number of projects that displaced mountain families in this region.

Hungarian-born architect Roland Wank designed Norris Dam. Wank cared not only about the function of the dam, but its appearance as well. He considered the placement of overlooks on either side of the dam and designed a visitors center. The dam was proportional; carefully placed window openings and the placement of the formwork boards created texture and pattern.

Today, Norris Dam is part of Norris Dam State Park (125 Village Green Circle, Lake City, 865/426-7461 or 800/543-9335). Visitors may see the picturesque dam from overlooks on both sides of the lake; U.S. 441—the main thoroughfare in the park—tracks along the top of the dam. It is an impressive sight. The visitors center, on the east side of the dam, has public restrooms and displays about construction of the dam.

Norris Dam is also home to the **Lenoir Museum** (865/494-9688, Wed.–Sun. 9 A.M.–5 P.M., free), named for Will G. Lenoir, a local resident who amassed a mind-boggling collection of mountain artifacts during his lifetime. Lenoir traveled the back roads of East Tennessee to purchase housewares, old farm implements, mementos, and other remnants of everyday life of the early 20th century. When Lenoir died, he donated his collection to the State of Tennessee, and eventually the Lenoir Museum was built at Norris Dam State Park.

In addition to Lenoir's collection, the museum houses displays about Native Americans and the construction of Norris Dam.

Next to the Lenoir Museum are two authentic structures that were moved to the park during construction of TVA dams and lakes. The **Caleb Crosby Threshing Barn** once sat on the Holston River where the David A. Green Bridge now spans Cherokee Lake on Highway 25 East. Before the lake flooded the farm site, the barn was carefully dismantled and put in storage, where it was kept for 34 years until 1978, when it was reconstructed at Norris Dam.

Next to the threshing barn is the **18th Century Rice Gristmill,** originally constructed in 1798 by James Rice along Lost Creek in Union County. Four generations of the Rice family operated the mill from 1798 until 1935,

the 18th Century Rice Gristmill at the Lenoir Museum Cultural Complex

when TVA bought the land on which it sat in preparation for flooding of Norris Lake. The Civilian Conservation Corps labeled all the components of the mill, disassembled it, and reassembled it on its present land. During the summer, park staff still operate the mill and have gift items for sale.

Recreation

Despite its rich history, most people come to Norris Dam State Park to relax and enjoy the outdoors. Boating and fishing are popular on the Clinch River and on Norris Lake, in part because the water is so deep and cool, and the fish so plentiful. There are several licensed commercial marinas (865/494-8138) on the lake, including ones where you can rent houseboats for your stay. There are 15 miles of hiking trails and another 15 miles of multiuse dirt and gravel paths ideal for biking. An Olympic-size swimming pool is open during the summer Wednesday–Sunday 10 A.M.–6 P.M.

Cabins and Camping

Norris has 19 rustic cabins (865/426-7461, $60–85) and 10 three-bedroom deluxe cabins ($70–105). All cabins are located in a wooded setting and have kitchens, bathrooms, fireplaces, linens, and outdoor picnic tables and grills. The Norris campground has 75 sites ($20) with electrical and water hookups. Houseboat rates vary by season, size of boat, and availability.

OLIVER SPRINGS

The town of Oliver Springs is just a blip on the map, but it's worth stopping to see the general store, the library (housed in the old train depot), and the town hall.

The real reason people head to Oliver Springs, though, is to get to the **Coal Creek OHV Area and Windrock Park** (865/435-1251, www. coalcreekohv.com). The park offers more than 72,000 acres of wide-open spaces, including trails, camping, cabins, and fantastic scenery.

KNOXVILLE

COURTESY OF ANDERSON COUNTY TOURISM COUNCIL

There are 72,000 acres of off-road fun at Coal Creek OHV Area and Windrock Park.

OAK RIDGE

America created the atomic bomb—or parts of it, at least—at the Y-12, X-10, and K-25 plants in this city, northwest of Knoxville. Talk about top secret! Even those involved didn't really know what was happening, and The Secret City moniker remains one people use. Today, Oak Ridge and its plants are still an important component in the national defense industry. Oak Ridge's heritage is part of everything in the city. You can sense how smart everyone in town is (the government recruited the best and brightest to work here, and many of their off-spring have stayed): This is a little brain trust in the mountains. You can't walk away from here without a different perspective on the country.

History

Oak Ridge did not exist before 1942. When nuclear fission was discovered in the late 1930s, American scientists warned that this technology could be used to create a weapon more powerful than any known to man. As World War II escalated, and the United States joined the conflict in 1941, the U.S. military decided to exploit this technology. Sites in New Mexico, Washington state, and East Tennessee were chosen for the work. The isolated hills in Tennessee were chosen because they were close to roads and rail lines, they had ample supply of electricity, and they would be hard for spies and the curious to discover. Before the land was taken over by the government, about 3,000 people lived in homes that were scattered around the hills and valleys. Each homeowner received a letter stating that their land and home were being taken, and how much money they would receive in exchange.

Oak Ridge was built seemingly overnight. Between the spring of 1943 and the fall of 1944, the 59,000-acre tract of land bought for the project was developed into 10,000 homes and apartments, 13,000 dormitory spaces, 5,000 trailers, and more than 16,000 barracks. One of the facilities, K-25, where they processed uranium, was at the time the largest building in the world under one roof. Workers rode bicycles to get from one side of the massive structure to the other.

Social societies, schools, churches, theaters, barber shops, and much more were developed to entertain and meet the needs of the new residents.

When the United States dropped atomic bombs in Hiroshima and Nagasaki on August 6 and September 2, 1945, many workers at Oak Ridge learned for the first time what they had been doing all this time. Many believed and were proud that they had helped to end World War II.

The end of the war did not mean the end of Oak Ridge. Y-12 continues to research, develop, and produce weapons for the U.S. military. In 1948, X-10 became the Oak Ridge National Laboratory, a center for science and research managed successively by the University of Chicago, Monsanto Chemical, Union Carbide, and Lockheed Martin corporations. It is now managed by the University of Tennessee and Battelle, and remains a center for scientific research in a wide range of fields.

American Museum of Science and Energy

Oak Ridge's premier attraction is the American Museum of Science and Energy (300 S. Tulane Ave., 865/576-3200, www.amse.org, Mon.–Sat. 9 a.m.–5 p.m., Sun. 1–5 p.m., adults $5, seniors $4, children 6–17 $3). The museum serves double duty: It houses an exhibit about the development of Oak Ridge, and it is a science museum for young people. The historical exhibit relies on newspaper clippings, original documents, and audiovisuals to describe Oak Ridge during World War II. The science museum has features dedicated to types of energy, including nuclear.

◖ Oak Ridge National Laboratory

Before September 11, 2001, visitors were allowed walk-in tours of Y-12/Oak Ridge National Laboratory (865/574-7199, www.ornl. gov). But in today's security-anxious world, casual visitors are not allowed on the campus of the nuclear plant without an advance reservation. Call to arrange a tour, or get on one of the public bus and train tours offered in collaboration with the American Museum of Science and Energy (AMSE). These tours run daily June–September. To get on board the bus tour, you must sign up in person at the AMSE before 9 a.m. on the day of the tour. The bus leaves at noon and returns at about 3 p.m. The bus tour is free with paid admission to the museum.

If you're short on time or don't want to get tangled up at the AMSE, then head for the **K-25 overlook** (Highway 58), a minimuseum and viewing station located about 10 miles south of Oak Ridge. You'll drive through the city's industrial park before arriving to the overlook. Inside a small enclosed building is a short version of Oak Ridge's history. Outside you can see the K-25 plant as well as other Oak Ridge infrastructure. It is not scenic, but it's still a view.

Across from the K-25 Technology Park is the **Wheat African Burial Ground,** which houses 90 unmarked graves believed to be those of slaves from the Wheat Plantation. The cemetery dates back to 1850.

Other Sights

While most of "old Oak Ridge" has been razed and rebuilt in the ubiquitous modern American style of strip malls and parking lots, parts of the city date back to the 1940s. **Jackson Square** remains largely unchanged since it was built as Oak Ridge's original town center. The low-slung horseshoe-shaped shopping center is home to professional offices, a few cafés, and the Oak Ridge Playhouse. Across Kentucky Street from the square are the remains of the **Alexander Motor Inn,** Oak Ridge's original and only hotel during the war. Above the inn is the **Chapel on the Hill,** a church that served as the place of worship for numerous denominations during the war.

Other don't-miss attractions in Oak Ridge include the **International Friendship Bell,** located downtown, which is a monument to peace. The **Secret City Commemorative Walk,** also downtown, is a memorial to the 75,000 men and women who built Oak Ridge during the 1940s.

The **Children's Museum of Oak Ridge** (461 W. Outer Dr., 865/482-1074, www. childrensmuseumofoakridge.org, Tues.–Fri. 9 A.M.–5 P.M., Sat. 10 A.M.–4 P.M., Sun. 1–4 P.M., adults $7, seniors $6, children 3–18 $5) building was the Highland View Elementary School during the Manhattan Project era. Founded as a Girl Scout project in 1973, this is probably Tennessee's best children's museum, and it does a remarkable job explaining the area's complex history to even the youngest of visitors. In addition to The Secret City history, there's a child-size dollhouse, a rain forest, a bird room, a water flume, and a spectacular model railroad. Model-train buffs from Knoxville make the trek to keep this exhibit running.

When you've had enough Manhattan Project–era tourism in Oak Park, head to the **University of Tennessee Arboretum** (901 S. Illinois Ave., 865/483-3571, daily 8 A.M.–sunset). Here you can stroll through 250 acres of trees. There are a number of easy, self-guided walking trails, each well marked should you want to learn about the flora of the region. If you just want some time to commune with nature, that works, too.

Tours

The **Secret City Scenic Excursion Train** (865/241-2140, www.techscribes.com/sarm/srm_scs.htm, Apr.–Sept. first and third Sat., Oct.–Nov. selected weekends, Sat. 11 A.M., 1 P.M., and 3 P.M., Sun. 1 P.M. and 3 P.M., adults $17 children 4–18 $13, call ahead) combines pretty scenery with the history of Oak Ridge.

The train departs from Wheat Union Station, near the K-25 overlook on Highway 58. The journey travels a 12-mile route through the Manhattan Project site. The guides cram in a lot of information on these rides; the train will likely be of more interest to little ones than the lecture.

Entertainment and Events

The Oak Ridge Art Center (201 Badger Rd., 865/482-1441, www.oakridgeartcenter.org, Tues.–Fri. 9 A.M.–5 P.M., Sat.–Mon. 1–4 P.M., free) displays local and regional artwork. Exhibits change regularly and are fairly small. Getting a glimpse of the working studio is the appeal of this attraction.

Each June Oak Ridge tells its story during the **Secret City Festival** (www.secretcityfestival.com). There are World War II reenactments, live music, a juried art show, tennis tournaments, and plenty of activities for kids.

Food

For a meal in Oak Ridge, head to Jackson Square, where you can join the crowds at **Big Ed's Pizza** (101 Broadway, 865/482-4885, Mon.–Sat. 11 A.M.–11:30 P.M., $8–15), the city's most famous restaurant and a well-loved pizza parlor. Also on Jackson Square is **The Soup Kitchen** (47 E. Tennessee Ave., 865/482-3525, Mon.–Fri. 11 A.M.–7:30 P.M., Sat. 11 A.M.–2 P.M., $5–12), which serves excellent sandwiches, salads, and soups. Don't skip the Chilios (a combination of Fritos, chili, and cheese). End the meal with ice cream at **Razzleberry's Ice Cream Lab and Kitchen** (223 Jackson Sq., 865/481-0300, Mon.–Thurs. noon–8 P.M., Fri.–Sat. noon–9 P.M.).

With menu items including the Y-12 and K-25 breakfast specials, you know you are in Oak Ridge when you are at the **Jefferson Soda Fountain** (22 N. Jefferson Cir., 865/482-1141, Mon.–Fri. 7 A.M.–3 P.M., Sat. 6:30 A.M.–2 P.M., $6–10). Try the Myrtle Burger and stay long enough to hear longtime Oak Ridgers tell their tales.

Take in the scenery at the **Riverside Grille**

SAM HOUSTON: THE RAVEN

The word *colorful* does not do justice to Sam Houston, onetime Tennessee governor and one of the state's most complex and controversial citizens during the first half of the 19th century.

Born in Lexington, Virginia, in 1793, Houston was just 13 when his father died. His mother, Elizabeth, brought Sam and his eight siblings to Blount County, where he went to school for the first time and promptly memorized Pope's translation of Homer's *Iliad*. When his teacher refused to teach Houston Greek and Latin, the teenager disappeared from his family home. Houston traveled the rural mountainsides of East Tennessee and spent long periods in a Cherokee village. Oo-Loo-Te-Ka, a Cherokee chief, became a surrogate father to Houston and named him the Raven. Houston learned the language and ways of the Cherokee.

Some years later Houston needed to pay off debts, and in 1811 he opened a school in Blount County where he charged the then-astronomical fee of $8 per student per year. After about a year, when he was 20 years old and had paid his debts, Houston joined the army and quickly rose to an officer rank. Andrew Jackson noticed Houston's bravery and intelligence at the Battle of Horseshoe Bend during the Creek Wars of 1814. The future president stationed Houston to his regional headquarters in Nashville, and the young East Tennessean became part of Jackson's so-called Tennessee Junto, his political machine.

In 1819 Houston quit the army to study law and shortly after was appointed attorney general for Davidson County. Houston ran successfully for a seat in the U.S. House of Representatives, where he served two terms. In 1827 he was elected governor of Tennessee.

Houston's station at the top of Tennessee politics was not to last. He had a tumultuous private life, fueled by bouts of drinking and depression. While campaigning for his second term as Tennessee governor, Houston married Eliza Allen, the daughter of a prominent Middle Tennessee family. She left him after just 80 days of marriage, and Houston resigned the governorship and fled to the Cherokee, now living in Oklahoma.

So began the next chapter for Houston, who went on to marry a Cherokee wife, lead the Texas army against Mexico, and be elected president of the Republic of Texas. Later, in 1840, he married again, this time to Margaret Lea of Alabama, with whom he would have eight children. He worked tirelessly to achieve Texas annexation to the United States, which occurred in 1845. While Houston served as a senator from Texas from 1846 until 1858 he promoted the transcontinental railroad, criticized the army, and supported the Union. In 1859 Houston was elected governor of Texas, where he opposed the state's secession. He died in 1863.

Tennessee historian and writer Wilma Dykeman described Houston this way: "A strange, interesting combination of scout and scholar, woodsman and humanitarian, Sam Houston balanced Homer with humor and represented a sense of the total community of man."

(100 Melton Lake Peninsula, 865/862-8646, www.riversidegrilletn.com, Mon.–Thurs. 11 A.M.–9 P.M., Fri.–Sat. 11 A.M.–10 P.M., Sun. 11 A.M.–4 P.M., $4–18). Here you will enjoy steaks, salads, and a view of Melton Hill Lake.

Information

The **Oak Ridge Welcome Center** (102C Robertsville Rd., 865/482-7821, www. oakridgevisitor.com, year-round Mon.– Fri. 9 A.M.–5 P.M., June–Oct. also open Sat. 9 A.M.–1 P.M.) hands out maps and brochures, and helps travelers plan their visit to the city.

MARYVILLE

One of the oldest cities in East Tennessee, Maryville was named for Mary Grainger Blount, the wife of territorial governor William Blount. It is the home of Maryville College, a four-year college founded in 1819. Maryville College was among the first Southern schools to admit Native Americans, African Americans, and women.

On the northern outskirts of Maryville is Alcoa, established as a company town for the Aluminum Corporation of America in 1914. ALCOA remains an important economic engine for Blount County.

Sights

The **Sam Houston Schoolhouse** (3650 Sam Houston Schoolhouse Rd., 865/983-1550, www.samhoustonhistoricschoolhouse.org, Tues.–Sat. 10 A.M.–5 P.M., Sun. 1–5 P.M., adults 17 and older $5, children 9–16 $3) is the one-room schoolhouse where Sam Houston taught for about a year beginning in 1812. Houston, one of early Tennessee's most remarkable citizens, was mostly self-educated. Raised in part by the Cherokee, who named him Raven, Houston went on to be governor of Tennessee, president of the Republic of Texas, and senator and governor of the state of Texas.

The Sam Houston Schoolhouse was built around 1794 by area settlers who wanted a place for their children to be educated. Several different teachers held class in this little one-room schoolhouse until Houston's arrival in 1812. Houston, who took up teaching in order to pay off his debts, stayed for only a year. But his name has remained tied with the institution up to the present day.

Today, the Sam Houston Schoolhouse re-creates early schools on the Tennessee frontier. Reenactments can be arranged for groups.

Shopping

Southland Books (1519 E. Broadway, 865/984-4847, daily 10 A.M.–1 P.M.) is an excellent used-book store, popular meeting place, art gallery, and coffee shop. Stop in at any time for a pick-me-up pastry and coffee drink. Owner Lisa Misosky serves a special homemade lunch special every weekday.

Accommodations

Located at McGhee Tyson Airport is the **Hilton Knoxville Airport** (2001 Alcoa Hwy., Alcoa, 865/970-4300, www.hiltonknoxvilleairport. com, $150–190). Its 326 guest rooms offer work desks, high-end bedding, coffeemakers, and MP3-player plug-ins.

Food

Local chains include Knoxville-based **Aubrey's** (909 W. Lamar Alexander Pkwy., 865/379-8800, Sun.–Thurs. 11 A.M.–10 P.M., Fri.–Sat. 11 A.M.–11 P.M. $12), which serves pasta and steaks; there's also **Lemon Grass Thai Cuisine and Sushi Bar** (912 W. Lamar Alexander Pkwy., 865/681 8785, www.mylemongrass.com, Mon.–Thurs. 11 A.M.–3 P.M., 5–10 P.M., Fri.–Sat. 11 A.M.–3 P.M., 5–11 P.M., Sun. noon–10 P.M., $11).

www.moon.com

DESTINATIONS | ACTIVITIES | BLOGS | MAPS | BOOKS

MOON.COM is ready to help plan your next trip! Filled with fresh trip ideas and strategies, author interviews, informative travel blogs, a detailed map library, and descriptions of all the Moon guidebooks, Moon.com is all you need to get out and explore the world—or even places in your own backyard. While at Moon.com, sign up for our monthly e-newsletter for updates on new releases, travel tips, and expert advice from our on-the-go Moon authors. As always, when you travel with Moon, expect an experience that is uncommon and truly unique.

f 𝕏 KEEP UP WITH MOON ON FACEBOOK AND TWITTER
JOIN THE MOON PHOTO GROUP ON FLICKR

MAP SYMBOLS

▦▦▦	Expressway	◖	Highlight	✕	Airfield	⚎	Golf Course
▦▦	Primary Road	○	City/Town	✈	Airport	🅿	Parking Area
▦	Secondary Road	◉	State Capital	▲	Mountain	⬛	Archaeological Site
⋯	Unpaved Road	✹	National Capital	✚	Unique Natural Feature	⬘	Church
------	Trail	★	Point of Interest			⬛	Gas Station
⋯⋯	Ferry	•	Accommodation	🌫	Waterfall	⬭	Glacier
⌁⌁	Railroad	▾	Restaurant/Bar	⬙	Park	▨	Mangrove
▦	Pedestrian Walkway	▪	Other Location	⬛	Trailhead	▨	Reef
⫿⫿	Stairs	⋀	Campground	⚶	Skiing Area	▭	Swamp

CONVERSION TABLES

°C = (°F – 32) / 1.8
°F = (°C x 1.8) + 32
1 inch = 2.54 centimeters (cm)
1 foot = 0.304 meters (m)
1 yard = 0.914 meters
1 mile = 1.6093 kilometers (km)
1 km = 0.6214 miles
1 fathom = 1.8288 m
1 chain = 20.1168 m
1 furlong = 201.168 m
1 acre = 0.4047 hectares
1 sq km = 100 hectares
1 sq mile = 2.59 square km
1 ounce = 28.35 grams
1 pound = 0.4536 kilograms
1 short ton = 0.90718 metric ton
1 short ton = 2,000 pounds
1 long ton = 1.016 metric tons
1 long ton = 2,240 pounds
1 metric ton = 1,000 kilograms
1 quart = 0.94635 liters
1 US gallon = 3.7854 liters
1 Imperial gallon = 4.5459 liters
1 nautical mile = 1.852 km

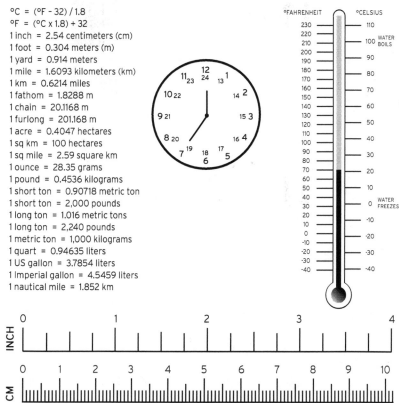

MOON SPOTLIGHT
CHATTANOOGA & KNOXVILLE
Avalon Travel
a member of the Perseus Books Group
1700 Fourth Street
Berkeley, CA 94710, USA
www.moon.com

Editor: Leah Gordon
Series Manager: Kathryn Ettinger
Copy Editor: Justine Rathbun
Graphics & Production Coordinator: Domini Dragoone
Cover Designer: Domini Dragoone
Map Editor: Albert Angulo
Cartographers: Kaitlin Jaffe, Heather Sparks

ISBN: 978-1-61238-153-4

Front cover photo: Boat on the Tennessee River in Chattanooga, © Denis Jr. Tangney/istockphoto.com
Title page photo: downtown Chattanooga and Lookout Mountain, © Melinda Fawver/123RF

Printed in the United States.

All recommendations, including those for sights, activities, hotels, restaurants, and shops, are based on each author's individual judgment. We do not accept payment for inclusion in our travel guides, and our authors don't accept free goods or services in exchange for positive coverage.

KEEPING CURRENT

If you have a favorite gem you'd like to see included in the next edition, or see anything that needs updating, clarification, or correction, please drop us a line. Send your comments via email to feedback@moon.com, or use the address above.

ABOUT THE AUTHOR

Margaret Littman

Margaret Littman is both an old-timer and a relative newcomer to Tennessee. After graduating from Vanderbilt University, she left Tennessee for points north over the course of her writing career. But after 17 years she could no longer resist the siren song of the Parthenon, bluegrass music, or fried pickles, so she returned to Nashville, where she writes about Music City, travel, food, pets, and more. An avid stand-up paddler, she loves being a day trip away from the Tennessee River to the south, Reelfoot Lake to the west, and Norris Dam to the east.

There's nothing Margaret loves more than telling natives something they didn't know about their home state. And with 75,000 miles on her station wagon already, she has lots of ideas for little-known places to listen to music, eat barbecue, paddle a lake, hike to a waterfall, or buy works by local artists.

Margaret's work has appeared in national and regional magazines, including *Wine Enthusiast*, *Entrepreneur*, *The Tennessean*, and many others. She is the author of several guidebooks as well as the Nashville Essential Guide, an iPhone app.

Margaret has loved lots of places she's lived, but the day she looked down and realized she was wearing cowboy boots in synagogue, she knew she had become a Tennessean.